P9-CEL-195

FROGS

A CHORUS OF COLORS

Sterling Publishing Co., Inc.
New York

JOHN L. BEHLER
DEBORAH A. BEHLER

FROGS
A CHORUS OF COLORS

FOREWORD BY CLYDE AND CHAD PEELING

A COMPANION BOOK TO THE ACCLAIMED TRAVELING EXHIBITION

*For my parents, Mildred and Luther, who gave me free rein to discover
the wonderful world of nature and nurtured that interest; and my sister,
Judy Howells, for putting up with my tarantulas and scorpions. –JB*

*For my family, for love and support that never waver; and my good friends,
especially Diana, who nudges me to do more and try to do it better. —DB*

A CHORUS OF COLORS

Published by Sterling Publishing Co., Inc.
387 Park Avenue South, New York, NY 10016
© 2005 by Sterling Publishing Co., Inc.
Distributed in Canada by Sterling Publishing
c/o Canadian Manda Group, 165 Dufferin Street
Toronto, Ontario, Canada M6K 3H6
Distributed in Great Britain by Chrysalis Books Group PLC
The Chrysalis Building, Bramley Road, London W10 6SP, England
Distributed in Australia by Capricorn Link (Australia) Pty. Ltd.
P. O. Box 704, Windsor, NSW 2756, Australia

10 9 8 7 6 5 4 3 2 1

Manufactured in China
All rights reserved

Photography and illustration credits are found on page 157
and constitute an extension of this copyright page.

Sterling ISBN 1-4027-2814-X

For information about custom editions, special sales, premium and
corporate purchases, please contact Sterling Special Sales
Department at 800-805-5489 or specialsales@sterlingpub.com.

Design: Richard J. Berenson
         BERENSON DESIGN & BOOKS, LLC
         New York, NY

FOREWORD

IN THE COURSE of our forty years operating a specialized zoo for reptiles and amphibians, we've created exhibitions featuring many different creatures: mambas, cobras, lizards, giant alligators, and gentle tortoises to name a few. But when our team of zoologists and designers began to think about a traveling exhibition featuring only live frogs, we were uncertain at first. We knew that frogs are visually charismatic and popular with the public. But beyond color and charm, could frogs tell a meaningful story and captivate audiences all on their own?

Early in our research all doubts vanished. Our eyes popped open to the astonishing range and diversity of these amphibians. Frogs sport an amazing variety of survival strategies and physical forms, ranging in size from tiny tree frogs to goliaths the size of a human infant. Many are more colorful than the most dazzling birds, and their skins produce chemical cocktails of dizzying complexity. Frogs communicate with sophisticated croaks, grunts, chirps, trills, snores, growls, whistles, and deeply resonating bellows. Their voices have filled the night with song since the dawn of the dinosaurs. Some frogs get around by jumping, but others hop, climb, walk, run, burrow, swim, and even parachute. They eat insects, worms, spiders, snails, fish, rodents, small birds, and other frogs. One species even eats fruits. And the reproductive diversity of frogs is unmatched among vertebrates. In short, frogs are among the most visually stunning, vocally pleasing, and adaptively remarkable life-forms on the planet.

And frogs are challenging to exhibit. They are delicate creatures that react quickly to changes in their environments. The needs of living frogs and the visiting public are often at odds. Marrying the two required the construction of elaborate habitats and careful selection of species. Many frogs are simply too shy or fragile for public display.

But among the more than five thousand species, there are some that thrive on exhibit. Waxy monkey frogs from South America, for example, bask on exposed branches during the day, their transparent eyelids concealing the fact that they're asleep. Tiny tropical dart frogs strut boldly, protected by their warning colors and toxic skins. Chinese gliding frogs adopt picturesque poses on limbs or window glass. The bumpy, mottled skins of Vietnamese mossy frogs inspire visual treasure hunts as they sit frozen on

patches of moss right under the visitors' noses.

"Frogs! A Chorus of Colors" is a traveling exhibition that premiered in 2003, and its popularity has been overwhelming since its inception. It has hopped across the country and back again, attracting crowds wherever it appeared. The exhibition showcases frog diversity with living examples, but it is merely an introduction. We hope it whets the visitor's appetite for more information.

This book, carefully crafted by our good friends John and Debbie Behler, is a wonderful resource to continue that journey. It is a testament to the wild world of frogs and their great variety of form, lifestyle, ecology, and niche. Collectively, the Behlers have invested more than

seventy years in conservation with the Wildlife Conservation Society. Like us, they have witnessed scores of vertebrates slipping into extinction—gone forever in nature. Frogs are no exception in this sad story. Their world is rapidly changing, and today as many as one third of the species are threatened with extinction.

The future for frogs does not look bright, but it does not have to be this way. There are compelling reasons for we humans to come to their rescue. *Frogs: A Chorus of Colors* tells their story. With our help, their calls in the night will continue to give us pleasure for many generations to come.

—Clyde and Chad Peeling

INTRODUCTION

A SPRING CHORUS

T HE DATE VARIES from year to year. It comes with little fanfare or forecast, any time from early March to early April. There may still be snow on the ground and skim ice on the ponds, but one warm, rainy night, the woods come alive with the magical, some might say deafening, sounds of wood frogs and spring peepers gathering to breed and lay their eggs. That's the time we know spring has really arrived in the northeastern United States, where we live.

It's difficult to believe that the ducklike, hoarse, clacking sounds are coming from a three-inch-long wood frog, and harder still to think that such high-pitched trills are emanating from the spring peepers, creatures not much larger than your thumbnail.

As we slowly cruise the back roads near our house in the suburbs, along small streams and temporary ponds, we can hear the chorus long before we actually see the tiny peepers and wood frogs hop on the wet pavement, single-mindedly intent on reaching a pool filled by snowmelt and winter rains.

Wood frog
Rana sylvatica

Opposite:
Spring peeper
Pseudacris crucifer

The spring peepers sound a lot like sleigh bells jingling, only louder. When they reach their destination, they perch at the water's edge on water-soaked logs and dead vegetation. The males inflate the vocal sacs under their chins and emit high-pitched peep, peep, peeps to attract mates. After breeding and laying eggs, these tiny frogs head back to their hiding places in the woodlands. If not for their loud spring chorus and mass gatherings, you would hardly know they exist.

The larger wood frogs are also on the move, crossing the same stretch of road on which we've witnessed such scenes on similar nights over the past twenty-five years. Hundreds of them mix with dappling raindrops in the beams of our headlights. Added to this show may be the silent but flashy enamel black spotted salamanders that migrate to the same breeding pond, their bright yellow spots matching the double line down the middle of the road. As we cruise

9

along, we play our annual role as amphibian patrol. Whenever we find a slow-moving amphibian on the roadway, we stop, help it off the macadam, and give it safe passage to the breeding site.

An Endangered Chorus

Sadly, it's becoming more difficult each year to find these harbingers of spring. New roads cut off frog migration routes to water, and housing developments and strip malls shoot up seemingly overnight where once there were woods and streams. Frogs and other amphibians everywhere are losing their habitats to development, pollution, and subtle changes in their environments, such as global warming. The presence or absence of these sensitive animals is a great indicator of the health of a habitat, indeed the health of our whole planet.

Equally as important, frogs are a foundation block in nature's food pyramid, they are insect specialists, and they provide direct benefits to human medicine and to the development of new generations of drugs to fight our ills. They may seem insignificant, one of nature's little beings that we take for granted, but besides being vitally important to the well-being of our environment, frogs are fascinating, often amazingly smart, and even fun. We've spent a lifetime watching them, studying them, and learning from them. Join us as we introduce you to the vast, varied, and very unexpected world of those odd little creatures called frogs.

—John and Deborah Behler

IT'S A

FROG'S LIFE

CHAPTER ONE

WHAT IS A FROG?

THEY COME INTO THE WORLD looking like very small fish, complete with tails and fins. They're restricted to water, where their tiny mouths allow them to eat only minute bits of food, like algae, pond scum, or even their deceased siblings. Then, amazingly, overnight they start to grow limbs. Leg buds begin to sprout from their sides. They grow a new, cavernous mouth, and ditch the tail and fins. Finally, they walk out of the water to reside on land, where they can eat a variety of food that perhaps only a frog could love: termites, mosquitoes, other frogs. They are an evolutionary marvel.

Frogs are among the oldest living creatures on our planet. They have endured through temperature and landscape changes that have destroyed other creatures. And they have steadily improved over the many million years of their history. In high school biology, we may have been taught that they were "lower forms of life." Yet, despite their low ranking on the scale of life, their simple body plan and adaptive behavior have allowed them to survive while other species have been lost.

Frogs are pretty amazing creatures. They start out life looking somewhat like a fish (opposite, bullfrog tadpoles with developing legs) and live completely in water. Then, as if by magic, they transform into the adult form, which can look like the short, squat Argentine horned frog (far left), the slender, graceful White's tree frog (near left), or the colorful imitator poison frog (above). When is a frog a toad? When it is a pink-bellied harlequin frog, *Atelopus flavescens* (pages 12–13).

Frogs are vertebrates, animals that have a backbone, like fish, reptiles, birds, and mammals—including man. They are also amphibians, a word that comes from the Greek *amphibios,* meaning a being with a double life. They've earned this name because most live on land or in the water at different times in their lives.

Frogs come in a great variety of sizes, shapes, and colors. Some are very big, over a foot long and weighing as much as seven pounds. Some are incredibly small, less than half an inch long. They can be green or brown, like the frogs we see hopping across the road at night. But they can also be bright red or orange or blue. They can be brilliantly striped, dazzlingly speckled or dully blotched to match the leaf litter where they live. There are about five thousand varieties, and scientists are finding many new ones each year.

Several hundred million years ago the ancestors of today's amphibians, our frogs, salamanders, newts, and caecilians, were among the most dominant creatures on earth. During this time in earth's history, which geologists have named the Devonian and Permian periods, the planet's landmasses were bunched together as one giant supercontinent called Pangaea. This supercontinent was located along the equator, and its climate was primarily tropical. The early animals that lived on this land were much larger than the ones we know today. Some amphibian ancestors probably reached fifteen feet in length. Imagine frogs the size of raccoons, salamanders as big as crocodiles!

A Fish out of Water

The most likely ancestors of very early amphibians were a group of ancient fish called sarcopterygians. These creatures had lobed fins, which means that their fins worked somewhat the same way our arms work. About 370 to 360 million years ago one of the first of these lobe-finned fish ventured out of the water onto land. This long-ago creature had paired moveable fins with features similar to legs, an early form of lungs as well as gills, and internal nostril development.

But though it had taken a crucial early step onto land, this primitive amphibian was not yet truly adapted to living there. It could move its fins, but it lacked the muscular apparatus needed to prop itself up and really walk.

What would make a fish migrate from the water, where it was comfortable, onto land where it had to struggle to move? There are advantages and disadvantages for a water creature to evolve adaptations for living on land. On the plus side, there was less competition for food, since reptiles, birds, and other vertebrates evolved millions of years later. And a creature adapted to both land and water could elude predators that operate only in water. Perhaps its habitat was drying up, and land survival was imperative. On the other hand, as an amphibian it would be vulnerable to dehydration. The vast majority of frogs still cannot live totally on land.

Researchers have not been able to find much in the way of fossil records for early amphibians, and nothing yet discovered directly links today's amphibians to these presumed early ancestors. The best-preserved fossils, of an animal called *Ichthyostega,* were found in Greenland, in geolog-

Hundreds of millions of years ago, the ancestors of frogs and other amphibians crawled out of the seas. *Ichthyostega*, a primitive amphibian, roamed on land about 360 million years ago.

ical deposits from about 360 million years ago. The landmass that is now Greenland was at that time located along the equator, and it had a moist, warm climate. *Ichthyostega* was already adapted to living for extended periods on land. It used lungs instead of gills as its primary means of getting oxygen. It had a strong skeleton, with a well-developed rib cage. And it was a tetrapod, meaning it had two pairs of functional limbs. It could actually walk on land.

What adaptations and changes occurred between *Ichthyostega* and the first real frogs remain to be discovered, but at some point salamander-like ancestors of amphibians began to lose their long tail. The body grew somewhat shorter, and they evolved one of the most obvious characteristics of frogs. They developed the ability to hop.

The World of Amphibians

A unique group of animals in many ways, amphibians launched the beginnings of vertebrate life on land, holding their evolutionary place between fish and reptiles. Amphibians were the first vertebrates to develop tongues. Because they could now feed on land, out of the water, amphibians needed to be able to moisten their food so they could swallow it. They evolved eyelids, again to keep those organs moist. Amphibians also developed true ears, a larynx for making sounds, and a pair of structures on the roof of the mouth, called the Jacobson's organ, for sampling fluids and deciphering chemicals. Their skin is soft, moist, and unprotected by scales or hair.

Caecilians look like large earthworms or snakes, but they are amphibians. These secretive animals, such as this purple caecilian from Central America, live in water or underground in tropical regions.

Missing Link?

Recently scientists began looking at a two-and-a-half-inch-long bone that was found during the 1990s in red sandstone sediments in Pennsylvania. They believe it may have come from a new species that could represent the critical evolutionary route from fish to amphibian. This area in the north-central part of Pennsylvania is rich in vertebrate fossils from the geological period known as the late Devonian (about 400 million years ago). According to paleontologists at the University of Chicago and the Academy of Natural Sciences, the bone may have come from the upper arm of a three- to four-foot-long salamander-like creature. The bone had indications of well-defined muscular attachments at the shoulder and elbow, so the animal's forelimbs could have been strong enough to hold its head up out of the water. The scientists are closely examining the fossil for clues as to when the fin-to-limb transition took place.

There are more than 5800 living amphibians known to herpetologists (scientists who study reptiles and amphibians), and undoubtedly many more to be discovered. These modern-day amphibians fall into three categories.

The smallest group is the Gymnophiona (Apoda), or caecilians, with about 170 species. Legless, blind, and with segmental, ringed bodies, caecilians look rather like large earthworms. They are secretive creatures who spend most of their lives in water or in underground burrows.

Of today's amphibians, the salamander looks the most similar to the ancient amphibians—with a long body, four legs, and a well-developed tail. Like this spotted variety of North America, salamanders live mainly in temperate regions.

The next largest group is the Caudata (Urodela), or tailed amphibians—salamanders and newts—with about 540 species. Some species of salamanders are totally aquatic; others are terrestrial but live near water, since moisture is essential to salamander survival.

The third group of amphibians is our subject: frogs and toads. Called the Anura, the tailless amphibians, it has the most species, about 5100 in thirty families spread almost around the world.

The Naming of Frogs

With all those frogs, it's a job to keep them straight when speaking or writing about them.

For example, everyone in America knows the common name of the largest frog in our country, the one that sits at the edge of the lily pond and sings "Jug–o–rum." It is the bullfrog, of course.

However, for people in other parts of the world, that common name refers to entirely different creatures. "Bullfrogs" in South America, Africa, and Australia are not the same frogs that

The Scientific Name Game

Most frogs have a common name, such as bullfrog, tree frog or horned toad. But common names can vary from place to place, so scientists have their own, more precise system of naming and classifying frogs, and all other organisms. It's called taxonomy, and it is more than a simple filing system. It is a way to set down the relationship between all known creatures.

The classifications are the subject of some debate among scientists, but generally they are the same ones we learned in biology class. Going from the broadest to the most specific, they are: kingdom, phylum, class, order, family, genus and species.

Interestingly, frogs and man are in the same kingdom and phylum. Both are in the Animalia kingdom and the Chordata phylum. We even share a sub-phylum: vertebrates. But from thereon man and frogs diverge. Frogs are further classified this way:

Class: Amphibia, creatures adapted to both water and land

Order: Anura, which means "without tails"

Family: Determined by the frog's internal and external anatomy, breeding habits, body design of the tadpole, and other factors. There are approximately thirty different families of frogs, but the number is continually shifting as new information becomes available.

Genus: A more specific designation, based on more narrowly defined characteristics of body type, breeding habits, etc. There are approximately 360 frog genera.

Species: Frogs of any one species share the major characteristics of the family and genus into which they fall, plus other features unique to their group. There are approximately 5100 species of frogs, but this number is also in flux as new species are identified and old species are shifted to different families.

are sitting by America's ponds. And not only are they different from the North American bullfrog, but they are a different frog in each country. So if an African and an Australian happened to fall into a conversation about bullfrogs, they would not be speaking of the same creatures at all.

To herpetologists, it makes little difference what a frog's common name is. They have their own, more precise, system of names.

When a new frog is discovered, it is placed first in an umbrella group called a family. The scientist who describes the frog then gives it a unique Latin name composed of two words: genus and species. This is called the binomial system for naming. It was created by the Swedish botanist Carl Linnaeus in the mid-1700s and is still used today. It's a way of consistently naming a frog, or any other creature, and clearly differentiating it from similar creatures.

The species name is given to a group of frogs that share all the characteristics of the family and genus they are in, plus another set of characteristics not seen in related species. A genus always has at least one species, but it may include many

FROGFACT Common names of frogs can vary from one place to another, so to be specific, scientists use the frog's scientific name, made up of its genus and species. The genus is always capitalized and the species is lowercased. For example, the scientific name for America's bullfrog is *Rana catesbeiana*, meaning the frog is in the *Rana* genus and its species is *catesbeiana*.

species, all creatures that are closely related to each other somehow.

When writing the name of a frog, the genus is always capitalized and the species is always lowercased. So that large American frog we were talking about earlier is in the Ranidae family. (Family names always end in ae.) It is in the *Rana* genus, and its species is *catesebeiana*. The South American bullfrog is in the Leptodactylidae family. Its genus is *Leptodactylus* and its species is *pentadactylus*.

When communicating with each other, herpetologists usually refer to creatures only by their genus and species, so the American bullfrog is called *Rana catesbeiana*. The South American bullfrog is *Leptodactylus pentadactylus*.

With this system, neither the country where the frog is found, or the language being spoken

The Key to the Kingdom

In the taxonomy of life, man and frogs share a basic relationship. They belong to the same kingdom and phylum. Both are members of the animal kingdom and the phylum of animals with spinal cords. They share similarities of life processes, but their taxonomic relationship drifts in different directions and they occupy different classes, orders, and families. Frogs are amphibians, "cold-blooded," and usually lay jelly-coated eggs in water. There are more than 5100 species of frogs. Man is a mammal, a warm-blooded animal, and a primate. Primates bear their young alive. The hominids include man and his closest cousins, gorillas and chimps. And the species of man, *Homo sapiens*, is you and me.

	Wood Frog	Man
KINGDOM:	Animalia	Animalia
PHYLUM:	Chordata	Chordata
CLASS:	Amphibia	Mammalia
ORDER:	Anura	Primates
FAMILY:	Ranidae	Hominidae
GENUS:	*Rana*	*Homo*
SPECIES:	*Rana sylvatica*	*Homo sapiens*

makes any difference. *Rana catesbeiana* always refers to *Rana catesbeiana,* that big bullfrog sitting down by a pond somewhere in North America.

Finding Frogs

Frogs, as every little boy knows, are not difficult to find. They live just about everywhere, on every continent except Antarctica. They do not like extremes of hot or cold, but they can be found at almost all altitudes, from sea level to above 26,000 feet. Many frogs are terrestrial, living on or burrowing under the ground. Others are arboreal, and spend most of their lives in trees. At least two species, the North American wood frog, *Rana sylvatica,* and the European common frog, *Rana temporaria,* can be found within the Arctic Circle, but the majority are tropical and subtropical.

From Fish to Frog

Most frogs hatch from eggs into fishlike larvae, which are called tadpoles. During the aquatic tadpole stage, which can last for days or years depending on the species, frogs live solely in water. To breathe, newly hatched tadpoles have a pair of visible, feathery gills, one on each side of the body.

Adult frogs are easily recognized by their unique body design. The body is much shorter than those of other amphibians. The head is flush with the body, and there is no distinct neck. True to their order, frogs have no tails. In the Pacific Northwest there are two so-called tailed frogs in the genus *Ascaphus,* but the "tail," which only the males have, is actually a short copulatory organ used to fertilize the eggs of the female internally. This protuberance is the same color and texture as the frog's back and does look just like a tail, but it's not.

In frogs the nostrils and eyes usually sit on top of the skull, which means the animals can sit in water and still breathe and see while the rest of their body is hidden from predators.

The paired front limbs are short, and the hind limbs are marvelously well adapted for a lifestyle of jumping. On the two hind feet there are five toes; the ankle bones are elongated for increased leverage, and the leg bones are long.

Most—not all—frogs have teeth, but they are small and are nearly always located in the upper jaw. A few species also have teeth in the lower jaw. The teeth primarily aid in holding prey, and they are shed and replaced throughout the frog's life. Some frogs have additional rows of teeth on the roof of their mouth, called vomerine teeth, and a few have bony projectiles, like tusks, that protrude from the lower jaw.

Not So Cold-Blooded

We often call frogs and other amphibians cold-blooded. A more accurate term is ectothermic, which means that these

> **FROGFACT** In the Native American culture of the Southwest, the frog carries a piece of wood in its mouth because the Mojave people believe the frog helped to bring fire to humans. According to folklore, in the long ago Coyote stole fire from the selfish Fire Beings, mythological entities who were keeping the precious warmth for themselves. Coyote passed fire on to Frog, who was carrying it when the pursuing Fire Beings grabbed his tail. Frog tore himself free but left his tail behind. That's why frogs have had no tail ever since.

Muscle Mania

What difference does frog behavior mean to man? Maybe a lot. The green-striped burrowing frog, *Cyclorana alboguttata,* can stay buried in mud for months at a time. Yet, when it emerges, the frog suffers little effect from having been completely inactive. Scientists in Australia are studying this frog to understand its ability to maintain muscle mass despite long periods of starvation. Their findings could lead to the development of new ways to improve livestock production during droughts and to address muscle strength in older and bedridden humans as well as in astronauts, who suffer muscle wasting during their space flights.

The Long and the Short of It

The world's largest frog is the goliath *Conraua goliath,* of West Africa. Measured from snout to vent (the anal outlet), this species may exceed twelve inches in length and weigh about seven pounds. North America's largest frog is the bullfrog, *Rana catesbeiana.* It can grow to six inches and can weigh more than one pound.

There is some debate over the world's smallest frog. The Monte Iberia frog from Cuba, *Eleutherodactylus iberia,* and the gold, or flea, frog of Brazil, *Psyllophryne didactyla,* compete for the title at less than half an inch.

The largest toad is the marine toad, *Bufo marinus,* at up to ten inches and four pounds. It is native to Central and South America. Also known as the cane toad, it has been introduced in Australia, Florida, Hawaii, and other tropical and subtropical parts of the world, initially to control insect pests in sugarcane fields. Unfortunately, the marine toad adapts a little too well to these new environments. It breeds year-round in most places, and a single female can lay 30,000 eggs at one time. To make matters worse, the marine toad has done little to control the insects it was meant to keep in check and is now considered a pest itself. Most native frogs and toads are no match for this big toad, which consumes them with little hesitation. It also produces a toxin that can cause temporary paralysis or even death in dogs and other small mammals.

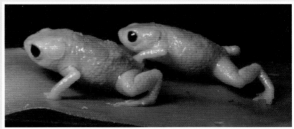

Frogs range in size from the goliath frog of Africa (top), which can measure more than twelve inches in snout-to-vent length, to the gold frog of Brazil at less than half an inch (above). The marine toad (left) can grow to a formidable ten inches.

Frog versus Toad

What is the difference between frogs and toads? There's a simple answer to this question. All toads are frogs, meaning they fall into the same group of amphibians, the Anura. But most people think of toads as being those big warty creatures with the dry skin, while frogs are smooth-skinned and slimy.

When naturalists of that day began to identify the wildlife around them, the animal they called a "frog" is the one we know today as the European common frog, *Rana temporaria*. It is the "typical" frog—with green and brown moist skin, a streamlined body, and long legs designed for jumping—and is classified with others of its kind in the family Ranidae, which are known as the true frogs.

Likewise, those early naturalists called today's European toad, *Bufo bufo,* a "toad." It was easily differentiated from the animal they called a frog by its warty, dry skin, stocky body, and short hind legs, made for short hops rather than the long leaps and bounds of the frog. *B. bufo* and other "typical" toads, the ones we picture when we think of toads, are in the

family Bufonidae, the true toads.

As European explorers voyaged to other lands and first saw the native anurans, they tended to refer to the smooth-skinned ones as frogs and the warty-skinned ones as toads. Some of these common names still stand, though scientists have learned so much about relationships and genetics that today we find warty-looking frogs and slimy toads. Some anuran groups have both "frogs" and "toads" in them, such as the Leptodactylids, which vary from the wide-mouthed Bell's horned toad (also known as the ornate horned frog), *Cera-tophrys ornata,* to the very un-toadlike white-lipped frog, *Leptodactylus albilabris.*

Frogs and toads all belong to the same taxonomic order and are collectively called anurans. In general, frogs (above, a pickerel frog) have moist skin, bulging eyes, and long, strong hind legs for jumping. True toads, on the other hand, are stockier, with shorter hind legs, and have warty, dry skin (left, a southern toad).

animals rely on their environment to regulate their body temperature. Birds and mammals, including humans, are endotherms. We generate heat chemically and internally by breaking down our food. It takes a lot of energy to keep our bodies warm. The bodies of ectotherms, on the other hand, reflect the surrounding air, substrate, and water temperature.

Some frogs alter their behavior to adjust their temperature—by moving from place to place or by positioning their bodies to expose a larger or smaller amount of skin to outside heat sources. The larger the frog species, the slower it is to warm up or cool down, because of its body surface to mass ratio.

In temperate climates frogs become inactive during cold weather, hibernating in streambeds, on pond bottoms, and beneath woodland debris. They may not be totally dormant at these times, however. Scientists have found that the northern leopard frog, *Rana pipiens,* is capable of swimming when it is disturbed in its underwater winter retreat.

Temperatures above 100° to 110° F are dangerous to frogs. Some species burrow during the hottest times of the day and in the summer, emerging only at night or during rains. This

> *FROGFACT* Have you ever seen a two-toned frog? When a green frog is sitting with its body half in sunlight and half in shade, it may look two toned, half dark green and half light green.

behavior is called estivation. Other species may remain underground for years, until cooling, rejuvenating rains arrive.

Skin and Color: More Than It Seems

The skin is a very important organ in amphibians, more so than in many other vertebrates. It's not just a protective cover. It also helps these animals breathe and maintain the water levels they need to survive. Its coloration hides them from enemy eyes, making them resemble the background in which they live.

Most frogs can change the brightness of their skin color, but not the color itself. Changes in brightness occur gradually and it is another way for frogs and other amphibians to regulate their body temperatures, since dark colors absorb more heat from the sun than do light colors.

Tomato frog, *Dyscophus antongilii*

Some species are counter shaded, with a darker color on the back to avoid detection from the air and a lighter shade on the belly so they are less visible to predators lurking underwater. Some tropical species match the bright color of the leaves on which they sit while others are dull brown, like old, dead leaves. In some species the sexes are different colors. The tomato frog, *Dyscophus antongilii,* of Madagascar is named for the bright red color of the female; the male is a duller orange. By contrast, the golden toad, *Bufo periglenes,* is named after the male's vivid gold-orange coloration; the female is black with scarlet blotches edged in yellow.

Frogs and toads cannot generate heat from within as birds and mammals do. Their body temperatures reflect their environments. To avoid overheating, some species of frogs, like this sandy burrowing frog, *Limnodynastes spenceri*, spend months underground in a deep burrow and emerge after a heavy rain to breed.

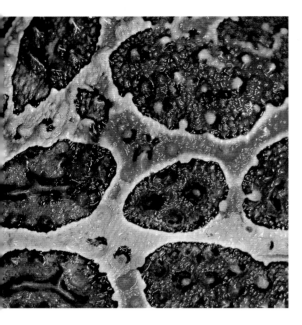

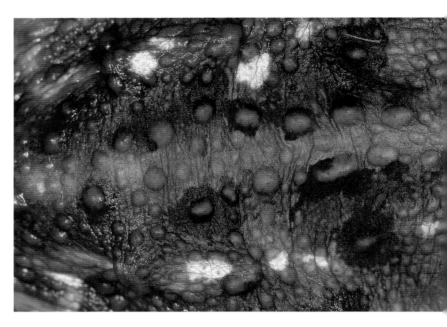

Layers of pigmented cells in the frog's skin control its color and pattern (below, a cross-section of frog skin with xanthophores containing orange pigment, iridophores containing reflective pigments, and melanophores, special cells that move dark pigments). Many frogs are masters of camouflage: Above, the mottled green skin of an Argentine horned frog helps it blend into its environment. Marbling in the skin of a marbled pygmy frog, *microhyla pulchra* (right) makes it difficult to see among the leaf litter on the forest floor. The "warts" in the skin of the marine toad (right, top) are really clusters of poison glands. When a predator grabs the toad, the glands secrete a toxic substance that will at least be distasteful and discourage the predator. Some frog toxins are so powerful they can kill a human.

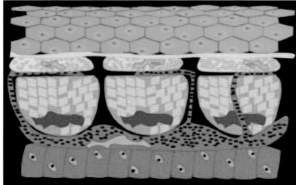

Some frog species exhibit a phenomenon called polymorphism, which means that a single species may have more than one color phase. The African reed frogs, *Hyperolius,* are good examples. Individual frogs of this genus may be striped, speckled, or plain, all living within the same population. Conversely, two striped individuals found in the same location may be different species of reed frogs.

Frogs also have mucous glands on the skin, which help keep it moist, and granular glands, which secrete toxins for defense against predators. The so-called warts on a toad's skin are really clusters of poison glands. While the toxins of most frog species are not very potent, they are distasteful and meant to discourage predators from eating the animal. Some frog toxins, though, are deadly.

As frogs grow and their skin becomes old, they shed the outermost layer of the epidermis by twisting and stretching to loosen it. The frog pulls its limbs out of the skin and then maneuvers the skin over its head—much as you would take off a sweater, except the frog does it with its mouth—and then swallows the skin.

Frogs and Water

Water regulation is as important to frogs as their body temperature. When they are on land, frogs and toads are continually losing moisture to evaporation, unless the air is highly saturated. That's why many frog species are found in the humid tropics.

Some frogs have evolved fairly sophisticated and interesting ways to avoid water loss. Take the waxy monkey frog, *Phyllomedusa sauvagii,* which lives in dry scrub forests in the Chaco Desert of South America. This small tree frog secretes a waxy substance. Using its arms and legs, it seals its skin by spreading the substance over its body, like a monkey grooming itself. During the heat of the day these frogs sleep in a sunny spot with their arms and legs drawn in. They hunt at night, when the

Unlike most other frogs, the Lake Titicaca frog lacks lungs. It lives high in the Andes mountains of Bolivia and obtains oxygen from cold water solely through its baggy skin.

danger of losing moisture is much less.

Water regulation is also important when a frog is in the water—taking in too much will create an imbalance of salts in the body. For that reason, many frogs cannot stay in water indefinitely.

Adult frogs breathe pretty much like humans; they bring in air through their nostrils or mouth, to the windpipe and into the lungs. But they can also take in oxygen through their skin, which has an extensive network of blood vessels. When frogs are submerged, their skin absorbs oxygen directly from the water.

But with frogs, there are exceptions to every rule. The Lake Titicaca frog, *Telmatobius culeus,* in

Frogs need moisture to survive. To keep their skin from drying out, waxy monkey frogs (above) cover their bodies with a waxy substance that they spread all over themselves—their own personal moisturizer and natural sunscreen.

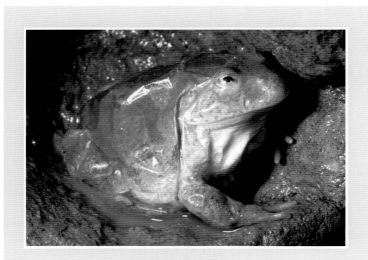

Hold the Water

The Australian water-holding frog, *Cyclorana platy-cephala*, lives in dry interior regions. It is a member of the tree frog family, but it spends much of its time burrowed into the soil. It can dig backward very quickly with its strong hind legs. Once in the burrow it forms a cocoon with its own shed skin to prevent moisture loss. This species also stores water in its bladder—and can survive for months and even years in droughts. When summer rains filter down to the frog, it eats its cocoon and emerges from the soil to breed in small temporary pools. Aborigines use this frog as a source of water.

skull, so the animals can see 180 degrees—in front, to the side, and partially behind them—but there can be a blind spot right at the front of the snout between the eyes. Frogs can retract their eyes back into the sockets, where they bulge against the roof of the mouth and help the animal swallow.

The pupils in most frogs are horizontal slits, but they may be vertical, round, or diamond-shaped, and they can be closed to a mere slit when exposed to bright light. Some frogs have specialized receptors to detect movement of small objects, such as insects. Often there's a translucent or transparent portion of the lower eyelid, called the nictitating membrane, which can be drawn up over the eye to protect it while the frog is in the water, but still allows a limited amount of vision.

Some frogs have brightly colored eyes, from lipstick red to metallic gold. In other species the eyes may reflect the skin color of the head or may be part of a pattern. Frogs and other amphibians, especially those that are diurnal, appear to have good color vision.

Bolivia, lives in the muck at the bottom of deep lakes at high altitudes. This species lacks lungs, but its skin is very loose, wrinkled, and folded, providing increased surface area for absorbing oxygen from water. At certain times of the year males of the West African hairy frog, *Tricho-batrachus robustus*, grow hairlike threads of skin on the insides of the thighs. These papillae also increase the skin surface area through which the frog absorbs oxygen as it searches for mates in the fast-moving mountain streams where it lives.

Why Frogs Have Such Big Eyes

Most frogs are nocturnal, so in order to see well at night, the eyes are large, protruding from the sockets, and in most species slightly inclined toward the front. They are also set high on the

The eyes of most frogs sit atop the head, the better to see with, even when sitting in water (below, a northern leopard frog). Frogs focus their eyes by moving the lens back and forth, like a camera lens (above).

Frogs have a nearly transparent nictitating membrane that can be pulled up over the eyeball to protect it while swimming. The frog's eardrum, called the tympanum, is located on the outside of the head, behind the eye.

Frogs Hear Really Well

Because male frogs establish territories and attract females by calling, hearing is an important sense. And it must be highly refined, so the female can discern the calls belonging to males of her species when several different frog species are chorusing from the same site. Most frogs have excellent hearing, but they cannot hear the highest or lowest sounds we humans hear.

Just as in humans, sound is received by the tympanum, or eardrum, and transmitted by small bones in the inner ear. In frogs, however, the tympanum is located on the outside of the body, behind the eye. When it comes to hearing, size matters: The size of the eardrums and the distance between them on either side of the head determine which sounds the frog hears best. In the American bullfrog, *Rana catesbeiana,* the tympanum of the male is twice as big as that of the female.

Speaking of Tongues

By and large, frogs are carnivorous, and many are what herpetologists call sit-and-wait predators—frogs who put themselves in places frequented by the insects, spiders, crustaceans, fish, and other creatures they eat. So in most frog species the tongue is attached at the front of the mouth, rather than the back, as in humans. When a delicious morsel happens by, the frog flips its conveniently placed tongue forward. Because the tongue is coated with mucus, the prey sticks to it and is drawn into the mouth as the tongue returns to its resting position.

Ear to the Ground

The Puerto Rican white-lipped frog, *Leptodactylus albilabris,* is a terrestrial, smooth-bodied frog whose mating call sounds like a chirp. When calling, the males often sit so that their throat pouches strike the damp ground with each sound. Scientists theorize that the thumps made by the inflated pouch produce seismic signals that may be alternatives to airborne sounds. In this way, the males may be able to make themselves heard over background interference such as the sound of the wind and calls from other frogs, particularly those of the arboreal Puerto Rican coqui, *Eleutherodactylus coqui.* Or the thumps may help signal how far apart the males are from one another.

A frog flicks its tongue at a passing mouse with deadly accuracy. The tongue is coated with mucus, so the prey sticks to it and is drawn into the mouth.

prey approaching, they immediately grasp it and pull it toward their mouth with their arms while thrusting their body forward with the hind legs.

High-Jumpers, Hoppers, and Burrowers

One look at the powerful, long, hind limbs of a bullfrog, and it isn't difficult to see why many frogs are superb jumpers. In fact, you can usually tell by the relative length of a frog's limbs what kind of locomotion it uses most. Species with long hind legs are generally jumpers; toads and other frogs with short hind limbs usually hop or run. Those with really stout bodies and short limbs are often burrowers.

Some frogs do not have tongues. Aquatic frogs in the family Pipidae, such as the Surinam toad, *Pipa pipa,* and the African clawed frogs, such as *Xenopus laevis,* are tongueless. To compensate, they use their arms and hands to bring in food. They sit motionless in the water, with their arms and fingers outstretched, and when they sense

A Record Jump from Rosie the Ribiter

Among Mark Twain's many famous works is "The Celebrated Jumping Frog of Calaveras County," published in 1865. It told a tale of life in Angels Camp, a California town that sprang up in the days of the Gold Rush. By the 1920s the streets of what was then called the City of Angels were in such deplorable condition that its citizens decided to pave the main thoroughfare. To celebrate the revitalization, the town held the first Jumping Frog Jubilee in 1928.

Today the Calaveras County Fair and Jumping Frog Jubilee is held in Angels Camp annually on the third weekend in May. The current frog jubilee triple-jumping record was set in 1986 by Rosie the Ribeter. An American bullfrog, Rosie jumped twenty-one feet five and three-quarter inches.

A South African sharp-nosed frog, *Ptychadena oxyrhynchus,* named Santjie, holds the world record for a frog triple-jump. Santjie jumped thirty-three feet five and one-half inches on May 21, 1977, in Natal, South Africa. Unfortunately, Santjie was not eligible for the Calaveras contest because he didn't meet the length requirement of four inches from head to vent.

Via slow-motion photography, scientists have discovered that in the act of jumping, the frog shifts its weight forward toward the short front legs, while the elongated ankles begin to unfold and lift the hind limbs off the ground. As the hind legs swing open from the pelvic girdle, the animal is propelled forward and upward. While airborne, the frog retracts its eyeballs into the mouth cavity, creating a more aerodynamic shape to its body. A similar technique is seen in aquatic species. These swimmers use their long hind limbs and large webbed feet to propel themselves through the water with a forward-thrusting motion. The Indian skipping frog, *Euphlyctis cyanophlyctis,* has the very remarkable ability to run on the surface of the water for short distances.

Arboreal frogs usually have skinnier, less muscular legs than other species, which allows them to efficiently walk along tree trunks and limbs. Tree frogs often have enlarged toe pads on their

Many frogs have long, muscular legs and are excellent jumpers. This bullfrog (above) leaps into water to avoid predators.

hands and feet. These pads are covered with tubular cells that, under pressure, compress and bend to fit the surface the frog is sitting on. Mucus on the tips of these cells helps them stick to almost anything, from a vertical tree trunk to a glass windowpane to the underside of a leaf.

Some arboreal frogs, like Wallace's tree frog, *Rhacophorus nigropalmatus*, of Malaysia and Borneo, can fly through the air with the greatest of ease. Actually, they are gliding or parachuting, rather than flying. These frogs have developed huge webbed feet. When leaping or jumping, the frogs flatten their bodies and spread the toes on all four of their appendages wide open. The webbing acts like the wings of a hang glider, slowing their descent, allowing the frogs to bank and soar between branches or parachute gracefully from high up in a tree to the ground.

CHAPTER TWO

WHEN FROGS GO COURTING

FROGS ARE SAID TO HAVE the most complicated reproduction process of all the vertebrates. But it's more accurate to say that their cycle is both simple and complex, depending on the species. For many it's a matter of the adults coming into breeding condition and meeting at a suitable site, such as a nearby pond, where they pair up. Then the females lay their eggs while the males simultaneously fertilize them. The adults soon leave the pond, and the eggs hatch into tadpoles, which metamorphose into juvenile frogs—and the cycle begins anew.

But the love lives of all frogs are not the same. There are frogs that lay their eggs out of the water. For those that do breed in water, not all do so in ponds or streams. Some breed in tiny pools in the centers of plants; others choose damp spots beneath fallen logs or in the holes of trees. Some don't lay eggs at all; they bear live young. Some species may not go through a tadpole stage, and in others fertilization may be internal rather than external. So, as with so much about these "simple" creatures, it's not that simple.

Breeding season is the only time you may see some frogs. During much of the year these animals are scattered around their habitat—feeding, hibernating, or estivating, depending on the climate and where they live. After frogs have become sexually mature, something triggers the adults to migrate to breeding sites. Three of the main environmental triggers are a change in the length of daylight, a rise in temperature, and rainfall. In the northeastern United States, for example, spring peepers are on the move on rainy nights in mid- to late March, the time of year when the days lengthen and temperatures begin to creep up from winter lows.

Frogs often return to the same breeding areas year after year. We're not sure how they find their way, perhaps by smell, familiar landmarks, magnetic fields,

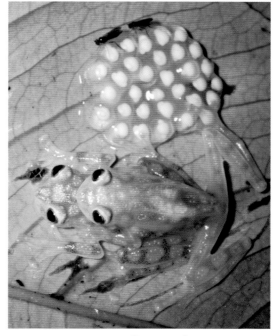

Many frog species mate in water and lay their eggs there (opposite), but other frogs and toads display a great variety of reproductive behavior. Above, a pair of reticulated glass frogs mate near an egg mass laid on a leaf.

Mating Double-Cross

The Amazon milk frog, *Phrynohyas resinifictrix*, breeds only in tree holes filled with water. The female lays her eggs in the pool of water and then leaves the male to fertilize them and care for the tadpoles. When the eggs hatch, the male lures another female to the same tree hole with his loud call. After this deceived female deposits her eggs, the male doesn't fertilize them, but instead feeds them to the tadpoles.

other sounds. For the most part, calls of small frogs are high-pitched, and those from big frogs are low-pitched. Couch's spadefoot sounds like a lamb bleating, the wood frog quacks, the carpenter frog's call is like a rhythmic hammering, and the American bullfrog has that familiar, deep harrumph.

Whatever the sound, the male's call, his advertisement, is music to the ears of the right female. Characteristics such as pitch, intensity, volume, frequency, and duration of the calls are important in locating mates, particularly in breeding areas that attract more than one species. The females need to identify a male of their own species out of hundreds of congregating and chorusing frogs.

The advertisement call telegraphs the species, sex, reproductive state, and location of the individual frog, all at the same time, and it can be loud. Scientists have recorded the call of the green frog, *Rana clamitans*, as audible for more than half a mile. The calls of some species may have components that "speak" to both sexes. The Puerto Rican coqui, *Eleutherodactylus coqui*, which is named for its call, is a good example. The *co* portion of this frog's call helps maintain space between the males, and the *qui* part attracts the females. Scientists have found that when two males are in proximity, they give only the first part of the call, and they may engage in a bout of aggressive *co* calls. The female, on the other hand, reacts only to the *qui* sound.

Female frogs will usually approach males

humidity, the position of the stars and other celestial bodies, the calls of other frogs, or a combination of some or all of these. Even if the site has been filled in or otherwise altered, the frogs may return there the following year.

Calling for a Mate

The first thing frogs must do when they arrive at the breeding site is to find mates. And they do that mainly by calling. Frogs were the first land vertebrates to develop vocal cords, and they have been calling enthusiastically ever since. In preparing to vocalize, the frog draws air into its lungs, closes its mouth and nostrils, and moves the air back and forth across its vocal cords. Many male frogs have single or paired vocal sacs, balloon-like structures under the mouth that act as megaphones to enhance the sound.

Each species sings its own tune. It could be a whistle, a trill, a croak, a grunt, a moan, a snore, or countless

FROGFACT The distinctive call of the Pacific tree frog—especially the mating chorus—is widely used in films for a "tropical" background. It is the only species in the United States that actually makes the familiar *ribbit* sound. Cartoon frogs are often given a Pacific tree frog voice as well!

In the majority of frog species, it is the male that calls. The advertisement call is made to attract a mate, but some males also call to identify themselves to other males or to protect their territories. Many male frogs have vocal sacs beneath their mouths that amplify the sounds they make (right, an American toad; top right, a green tree frog). The vocal sacs can be single or paired, as in the marsh frog above. The Puerto Rican coqui (below) is named for the call it makes. The *co* part of the call maintains space between males; the *qui* is what attracts the females.

silently, but some, like the American bullfrog females, will answer the males' advertisement calls with vocalizations of their own. They are usually soft in tone and audible over a short range.

A few frogs do not call at all. North America's tailed frog, *Ascaphus truei,* and some others that live in or close by streams and rivers are mute. This is another example of evolutionary accommodation to reality. There's not much sense in trying to call above the sound of rushing water.

In some frog species the males visually display to the females. The male Trinidad stream frog, *Colostethus trinitatis,* for example, jumps up and down on his perch to get a female's attention. A related frog in Venezuela, *C. collaris,* actually performs a courtship dance, in which the male crouches, crawls backward while swinging his body to one side, and leaps up on his hind legs, all the while increasing the rate and intensity of his call. Scientists have recorded as many as eighteen females watching one of these male frogs perform his little jig.

By contrast, when the female green-and-black poison frog, *Dendrobates auratus,* finds a calling male, she approaches and touches his snout with hers, places her front feet on him, and drums on his body with her hind feet—all this while the male is leading her to a site for egg laying. Then she leaves, and he tends to the eggs and transports the tadpoles to water on his back.

The green-and-black poison frog, *Dendrobates auratus,* mates during the rainy season, from mid-July through mid-September. Part of the mating behavior involves the female drumming on the male's body.

Timing Is Everything

Female frogs face a daunting situation, a biological "ticking clock" in the extreme. They have only about twenty-four hours during which their eggs are ready to be fertilized by the males' sperm. Mating generally takes place at night in waters filled with frogs of both sexes, making it difficult for receptive females to locate males in the short period of time they have, even though the males vocalize continuously during the breeding season.

The female African clawed frog, *Xenopus laevis,* has solved this time problem by making a clicking, or rapping, sound as her eggs become ready to be fertilized. This rapid series of loud clicks, similar to the sounds made by a Geiger counter when exposed to a lode of uranium, initiates a courtship duet with a nearby male.

Mating Embrace

Some frogs are explosive, cyclical breeders. They have only a short breeding season and come together in large numbers for a kind of, well, explosion, of mating. During early spring rains, for example, large numbers of North American wood frogs leave their woodland retreats. The males usually move first, gathering in ponds and temporary pools, calling to females, and grabbing anything that moves. Sometimes they even grab other males in error, despite the fact that females are usually bigger, especially when they are carrying a load of eggs.

Male frogs generally outnumber females at the breeding sites and will often fight for access to them. Like tiny sumo wrestlers, male golden mantellas, *Mantella aurantiaca,* will fight over breeding rights to an egg-bearing female. The two suitors, each only about one and one-quarter inches in length, try to flip one another over onto their backs. When a female appears, the male that remains upright wins the day. He goes over to her; she lays several dozen eggs, which he fertilizes.

Other frogs are prolonged breeders, meaning that their breeding period lasts for weeks or a month or even longer. In North America male bullfrogs and leopard frogs stake out territories, defend them against other males, and try to lure the females to their "pads." Many tropical species breed during the rainy season, which may last for several months. The males call every day, advertising their readiness, but the females are attracted to them only when their eggs are ripe.

When the male finds a suitable female, he first encircles her body from behind with his forelimbs and then holds her in an embrace, which is called amplexus. The exact position differs among various species.

Once the male frog has found a suitable partner, he clasps her in a mating embrace, called amplexus. Holding on to a slippery female frog in water is not easy. Here, a male golden toad clasps the female under her armpits. This species, *Bufo periglenes*, has not been seen in the wild since the late 1980s.

Typically, the male holds the female under her forelimbs. Some male frogs hug the female around her "waist," in front of the hind legs, or clasp her "neck" at the base of her head. Generally, in this piggyback position the female arches her back downward—signaling to the male that she's ready to lay her eggs—and elevates her vent. The male then brings his cloaca next to hers. As the eggs are laid, the male releases the sperm.

Holding on to a slippery female is not easy.

Sexually mature males of many frog species develop special structures, called nuptial pads, which consist of rough surfaces on the outer edge of each thumb. These pads enhance the male's gripping ability and help him hang on until the female lays her eggs. South African rain frogs are so rotund that amplexus is difficult, and the male secretes a sticky substance

Overleaf:
These two American toads could remain in amplexus for hours while the female deposits her eggs and the male fertilizes them.

from glands on his abdomen so that he literally sticks to the back of the female during amplexus.

Two species are known to engage in copulation. The males of both tailed frog species have a copulatory organ that allows internal fertilization. These frogs breed in cold torrent streams of the Pacific Northwest, and if there were no copulation, the eggs or sperm could be swept away before external fertilization could take place.

Lying in Wait for a Mate

While all this calling, dancing, and embracing is going on, "satellite" males often take up residence near or even right next to calling males. These parasitic males often remain silent, crouch down, and keep a low profile, but they position themselves so they can intercept females attracted by the calling males or take over the territories of those males once they have vacated them. A small but sexually mature male bullfrog may sit on the outskirts of a larger male's territory until he is challenged by the resident male or until the territory holder leaves. The smaller male may also move in and vocalize once the resident male is distracted by amplexus with a female, perhaps hoping to catch any late-arriving candidates. Some males, such as those of the northern cricket frog, *Acris crepitans,* have been known to alternate between calling and silent behavior.

There may be several advantages to this sneaky behavior. By being silent, the satellite male can be overlooked when a predator homes in on the calling male, and the satellite expends less energy when he is quiet.

Laying Eggs

The eggs of all amphibians are laid without shells, in layers of a protective, transparent, jellylike substance. These gelatinous envelopes hug the eggs and are inconspicuous at first, but they quickly swell, as water, oxygen, carbon dioxide, and waste ammonia flow freely through them. The envelopes are important protection, guarding the eggs against drying out,

ultraviolet radiation, physical damage, and perhaps even some predators. Generally, eggs laid in cold water tend to stick together in globs, and those laid in warmer water form thin sheets at the surface so they have better access to oxygen. Frogs lay clutches of eggs in clumps, and toads lay long necklace-like double strands of eggs.

Cluster or clump, the number of eggs in a clutch varies greatly: The tiny Cuban frog, *Eleutherodactylus limbatus,* lays a single egg; the wood frog lays from 2000 to 3000 in one clutch, and the cane toad and the bullfrog can deposit as many as 25,000 to 30,000 eggs at one time. Some species lay more than one clutch in a year; others, particularly those in dry regions, may emerge to breed and lay eggs only once every three or four years.

Some frogs have developed very sophisticated methods to keep their eggs safe from dehydration and predators. Foam-nesting frogs of the African savannas, for example, do not lay their eggs directly in water. During the mating season males and females gather near a pond in groups of as many as forty and climb a tree, where they crawl out on an overhanging branch. There, the females secrete a mucous substance, and both male and female frogs begin to kick with their hind legs, whipping the mucus into a white, foamy meringue. The frogs mate in the froth, lay their eggs, and then leave. The foam hardens on the outside, protecting the embryos from dehydration and predators. In a few days the tadpoles begin to emerge from their eggs and drop into the pond below to continue their life cycle.

To keep its eggs moist, the strawberry poison

Origami Frogs

As its name implies, Africa's leaf-folding frog, *Afrixalus delicates,* constructs a special nest for its eggs. While in amplexus the male and female draw the edges of a leaf together with their hind legs into a sort of pouch, where the eggs are laid. Secretions from the female's oviduct glue the leaf edges together. After the tadpoles hatch from the eggs, the leaf breaks apart, and they fall into the water.

Generally, frogs lay their eggs in water. The egg mass is encased in a gelatinous matter, which protects them from drying out, the sun's rays, and physical damage.

The life cycle of frogs begins with mating. Here, a pair of adult red-eyed tree frogs engages in amplexus while the female lays her eggs ① on a leaf above water. The tadpoles develop in eggs ② and fall into the water. There, the tadpoles begin to metamorphose into juvenile frogs, developing hind legs ③ and forelimbs ④. Not quite transformed into the froglet, a tadpole still retains its tail ⑤, but can cling to branches out of the water. The completely metamorphosed young frog ⑥ still lacks the striking coloration of the adult ⑦.

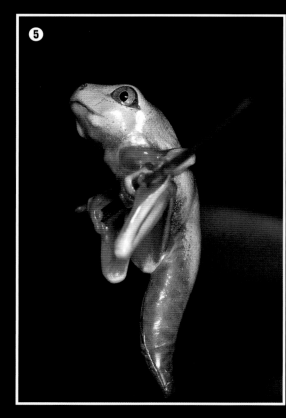

frog, *Dendrobates pumilio,* urinates on them. In addition, females of this species have been recorded transporting newly hatched tadpoles from nest sites on the forest floor to water-filled plants such as bromeliads, where the females release unfertilized eggs and feed them to the tadpoles.

The Tadpole Stage

After the female lays the eggs and the male fertilizes them, the embryos begin to develop into larvae, called tadpoles. Typically, tadpoles hatch from the eggs within a week to three weeks, but the development time varies. In some species it may last less than a week; in other cases it may exceed a year. But typically it lasts a few weeks or months.

Tadpoles look nothing like their parents. In fact, the typical tadpole looks a bit like a fish. It has external gills (usually three pairs), a lateral-line organ for sensing movement of prey and predators, a long tail, no legs, and a sucker on the underside of the head, with which it attaches itself to objects in the water. And much like fish, tadpoles often live in clusters, or schools, of similar-sized individuals. For the first few days tadpoles feed on the remaining yolk from the eggs; then they begin to feed on algae and other aquatic vegetation.

The Amazing Metamorphosis

As the tadpoles grow and mature, they begin to change into frogs in an amazing process called metamorphosis. Tiny limb buds form on each side of the body and start to develop into elongated hind legs. The front legs develop inside a chamber of skin that grows over the gills and

then break out of that covering. The larval mouthparts disappear, and the transforming tadpole develops jaws, teeth, and a tongue. The outer skin forms, and skin glands develop. Moveable eyelids appear, the tail shrinks and disappears, and lungs replace the gills. The vertebral column and limb bones harden, and a true stomach is formed. In addition, the long, coiled intestine, which is typical of herbivores and often visible through the tadpole's belly, shortens and transforms into a shorter gut typical of the carnivorous adult frog.

While all these changes are taking place, the frog is "neither fish nor fowl" and is extremely vulnerable to predators. As the front and hind legs are growing, its movements through the water are hindered. While its tail is being absorbed, it cannot hop or jump well to escape either aquatic or terrestrial predators. And the climatic conditions around it may change, endangering it further. Fortunately for many frogs, the metamorphosis process is relatively short.

The meadow tree frog of Costa Rica, *Hyla pseudopuma,* breeds in temporary pools and puddles that form during heavy seasonal rains. Its tadpoles must grow very quickly before the pools dry up. Sometimes they feed on their weaker sibling tadpoles to hasten their own growing process. Desert-dwelling spadefoots may complete their development and leave the water within two weeks. In contrast, the tailed frogs in cold mountain brooks can take three to five years to transform to the land stage, and bullfrog tadpoles spend one or two winters in ponds before becoming terrestrial frogs.

Some tropical frogs skip the aquatic tadpole stage entirely and develop directly in the eggs into tiny, fully formed froglets ready to go out on their own. There are even

The American bullfrog tadpole is large and takes much longer than tadpoles of many other frogs to completely metamorphose. It may overwinter for as long as two years before emerging as an immature frog.

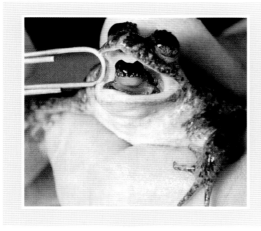

Unusual and Now Extinct

In the 1970s scientists in Australia discovered a new aquatic species called the gastric-brooding frog, *Rheobatrachus silus*. Living in fast-moving streams, the female swallows the eggs after they are fertilized, and they develop in her stomach. When fully transformed into frogs, they travel up to the female's mouth and sit on her tongue, then jump out and set off on their own. Within about ten years of its discovery, this species and a relative, *R. vitellinus*, disappeared from the natural habitat, and scientists believe they are extinct. No one is sure why they disappeared.

species, such as the Puerto Rican coqui, in which the female retains the eggs in her oviduct and gives birth to live young.

Parental Care

Amphibians in general deposit their eggs and then leave them to develop and hatch on their own. But a variety of frogs display degrees of parental care.

Some frogs literally carry their eggs to term. During amplexus the aquatic male and female Surinam toads, *Pipa pipa,* perform somersaults. At the peak of each rotation, while they are upside down, the female releases eggs and the male catches them on his stomach. Then with her hind legs, the female takes the eggs and pushes them onto her back, where they stay and are overgrown by skin. The eggs develop into fully formed toadlets while in these little "back pockets." The male Andean marsupial frog, *Gastrotheca riobambae,* catches the eggs as the female lays them; he places them in a special pouch on her back, where he fertilizes them. The tadpoles hatch in the pouch, and the female drops them into the water.

Among midwife toads, *Alytes obstetricians,* it is the male that carries the eggs. After the toads mate on land and the eggs are laid and fertilized, he holds on to the female and moves his hind legs back and forth until the strings of eggs are entwined around them. He carries this necklace of eggs for several weeks, returning to water every so often to keep it moist. When the eggs are about to hatch, he hops to a pool and releases the tadpoles.

After the female Darwin's frog, *Rhinoderma darwinii,* lays her clutch of eggs on land, the male remains nearby. When the developing young begin to move around in the eggs, he picks them up and holds them in his vocal pouch for several weeks until they are fully developed. Then he opens his mouth and the tiny frogs hop out.

FROGFACT In ancient Egypt, frogs were symbols of resurrection because of their remarkable metamorphosis from eggs to tadpoles to frogs. Frogs were carried as talismans and were often mummified with the dead as magical amulets to ensure rebirth.

The female Surinam toad carries her eggs in special "pockets" in the spongy skin on her back. The young develop there and hatch as fully formed tiny toadlets.

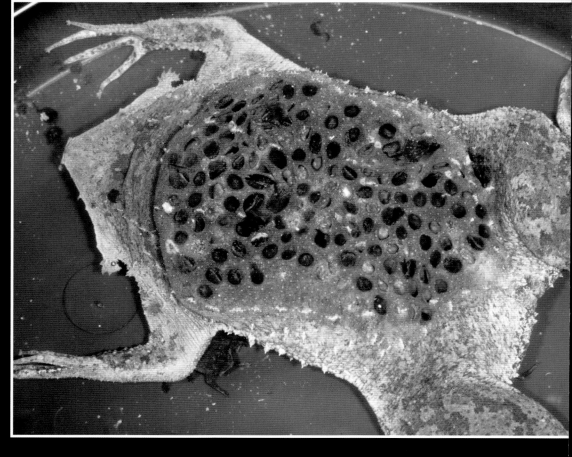

Once the female midwife toad lays her eggs and the male fertilizes them, he winds the strings around his hind legs and keeps the eggs moist. After several weeks, he takes the eggs to water, where the tadpoles hatch.

After the female Darwin's frog lays her eggs, the male guards them. When the tadpoles begin to move in the eggs, he takes them into his vocal sac, where they remain until he releases them as tiny froglets. This little youngster has just emerged from the male.

The female marsupial frog, *Gastrotheca riobambae,* has a brood pouch on her back into which the male places fertilized eggs with his feet. In this photo the tadpoles underwent direct development in the eggs and the young have emerged from the brood pouch as fully developed froglets.

CHAPTER THREE

IT'S NOT EASY BEING GREEN

AMPHIBIANS have had a long and successful history on earth. When they first ventured out of the seas to explore land, they had little competition in their new environment, since reptiles, birds, and mammals evolved millions of years later. So the amphibians flourished, and as they evolved into a dozen or more major groups they were able to colonize many different habitats.

Life, however, was not without problems. Amphibians had to deal with new and harsh climatic conditions—sun, dry air, and wind—that could rob their bodies of the water they still needed. Many of the early amphibians did not meet the challenges of life on land. And the ones that did make it have not been entirely successful in their struggles to conquer these hazards. Most must live in wetlands or moist habitats, or they must return to water to replenish their reserves, to breed, and to lay their eggs.

Today the surviving amphibians continue to face the same problems as their ancestors, as well as a whole new crop of problems caused by human activities.

Frogs at Dinnertime

Most adult frogs catch live prey and consume whatever they can stuff into their mouths and swallow. Gape size counts: big mouth, big prey; small mouth, small prey.

As for what specifically they cram into their mouths, it varies greatly. Frogs' eating habits run the gamut. Gluttons, picky eaters, generalists, specialists, cannibals, meat eaters, insectivores, and vegetarians—all describe the culinary habits of one frog or another and its tadpoles.

A frog's eyes are attuned to the slightest movements. Just a flick of an antenna can be enough to cause an insect to become a quick snack (opposite). Most frogs and toads eat live prey and whatever they can fit into their mouths, like this green tree frog with a katydid (above).

The familiar American bullfrog, *Rana catesbeiana,* for example, is a typical generalist. Bullfrogs are aggressive predators, and their diet may include scores of food items, such as fish, snakes, small turtles, small mammals, young waterfowl, and other small birds. But they aren't choosy, and their diet also includes small prey such as beetles, moths, dragonflies, spiders, crayfish, and snails. They eat smaller frogs too, which they locate by orienting to their breeding calls.

Other large frogs known for voracious appetites are the South American ornate horned frog, *Ceratophrys ornata,* and the African bullfrog, *Pyxicephalus adspersus.* Second to the goliath frog in size, the African bullfrog is also known for its fierce eating habits. Once, an African bullfrog was found in a snake enclosure in South Africa's Pretoria Zoo, where it had eaten seventeen newborn ringhals cobras in a single sitting.

At the opposite end of the feeding scale is the Mexican burrowing toad, *Rhinophrynus dorsalis,* a specialist that eats only ants and termites. In a prime example of ecological dependence this species lays its eggs in the partly flooded nests of leaf-cutting ants. The ants use the flooded area of the nest to deposit their refuse, and the particles they drop in are eaten by the developing tadpoles.

Then there is a real oddity in the frog world: Izecksohn's Brazilian tree frog, *Xenohyla truncata,* from the coastal lowlands of Rio de Janeiro. This is the only frog known to eat arum berries and coca fruits. Many seeds germinate better after they have passed through an animal's digestive system, and during this frog's wanderings, it deposits seeds and berries along with its dung, which serves as fertilizer. This unusual tree frog may contribute to the next generation of arum berries and coca in its community by aiding in seed dispersal.

Abundance of prey of the right size and type in a frog's territory often determines what the animal eats on any given day. The diet of a bullfrog that sits next to a lily pond differs from that of a bullfrog found near a sluggish river. Dragonflies and beetles may be the most common food at the pond, while crayfish and snails top the river menu. Crab-eating frogs, *Rana cancrivora,* which inhabit brackish water, consume mostly crus-

Fast Food

Couch's spadefoot toad, *Scaphiopus couchii*, is well adapted to North America's most arid climates. To beat the heat and sun-baked soils of the southwestern deserts, the toad spends most of its life underground. It may stay there for as long as three years before thunder, hard summer rain, and the low-frequency beat of raindrops on the soil above it stimulate the spadefoot to move to the surface. Its time aboveground is brief. It must breed quickly, before desert pools dry up, and it must find a large, nutritious meal. For the most part, the toad isn't too choosy about the bugs it eats, and it takes available crickets, ants, and spiders. It does, however, ignore blister beetles and stink bugs, which are armed with foul-tasting chemical defenses. At the same time the spadefoots are emerging, termites may appear in large swarms. This is a rare opportunity for Couch's spadefoot, and it may eat 55 percent of its body weight in termites in one sitting. After such a highly nutritious meal, the toad may go for a year before it needs to eat again. Some biologists believe that the presence of termites in the desert is essential for the survival of Couch's spadefoot.

The tadpoles of the red-eyed tree frog, *Agalychnis callidryas,* orient themselves in a vertical position in the water column and feed with their oral disc on suspended particles.

taceans, while those in freshwater habitats eat insects. The South African rain frog, *Breviceps verrucosus,* spends most of the year underground but comes to the surface after heavy rains. Its appearance often coincides with the swarming of termites, at which time there is a feeding frenzy; the nutrition the frog then derives will sustain it for many months underground.

Tadpoles: Magnificent Suction Pumps

Just as there are great differences in the feeding habitats of adult frogs, their larvae—tadpoles—vary greatly in how and what they eat. Frogs are remarkable among vertebrates because they start their lives as specialized filter-feeding tadpoles;

they suck in water and extract nutrition from the minuscule plants and animals they find there. Their body plan then changes dramatically during transformation to the land stage, when they become full-grown frogs.

For the tadpole, life is often a race against time. They have little protection during this period and must grow as rapidly as they can, all the while avoiding both terrestrial and aquatic predators. They do so in vastly different microhabitats—from temporary pools and ponds to

Tadpole Variations

Frog experts can identify a tadpole's species and habitat by examining its body shape and mouthparts. Most tadpoles are of the pond type—like North America's green and wood frogs, with prominent dorsal and ventral fins and thick tail muscles. They feed on algae, detritus, and leaves of aquatic plants. Stream-type tadpoles have reduced fins and a flattened body. In fast water, their large, sucker-like mouth helps them cling to objects, which they scrape for food. Terrestrial tadpoles undergo direct development on land in the egg and hatch as froglets. Other tadpole types are designed for feeding on surface scum, in open water, or eating other tadpoles (carnivorous).

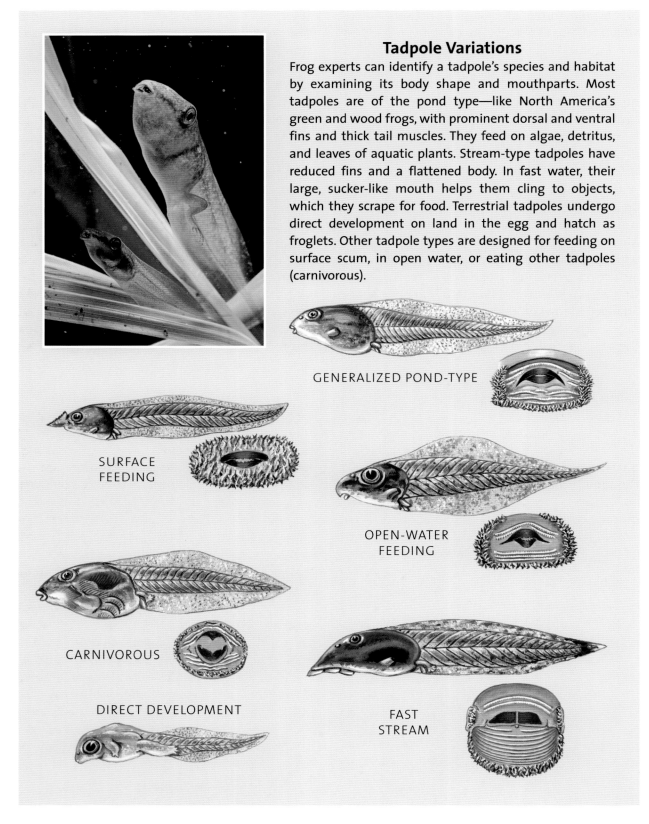

GENERALIZED POND-TYPE

SURFACE FEEDING

OPEN-WATER FEEDING

CARNIVOROUS

DIRECT DEVELOPMENT

FAST STREAM

brooks and torrential mountain streams—all of which require distinctive adaptations for feeding and locomotion.

Biologists can identify the species of a tadpole based upon the position, shape, and size of its mouth, and the body shape, tail musculature, and fin design. Each type of tadpole differs structurally in some regard from its kin. Tadpoles have been divided into two groups based on their eating habits: The ones that eat small particles are called microphagous, and those that eat large objects are called macrophagous. Tadpoles generally have ornate feeding structures around the mouth. Most often, these are in the form of an oral disc with papillae—small nipplelike protuberances around its perimeter. Hundreds of minute keratinized teeth—fingernail-like material—are arranged in rows on the tadpole's lips and serve as rasps, or scrapers, while keratinized sheaths on the jaws are used for biting, gouging, and cutting.

No matter what the tadpole eats, the same feeding mechanisms are involved. Most tadpoles have sievelike filter organs between the mouth and gills. These trap bacteria, unicellular algae, protozoa, and pollen grains that are suspended in the water that moves between the tadpole's pharynx and over its gills. A pumping action of the mouth maintains the inward flow of nutrients. These tiny particles accumulate on the mucous webs secreted by the tadpole's filter organs and are transported on mucous strands along a groove covered with cilia, or tiny hairlike structures, to the esophagus. Larger food items may travel directly to the esophagus.

Examination of the mouthparts, as well as other body characteristics, provides clues to the species' habitat and feeding strategy. The tailed frog, *Ascaphus truei,* of the Pacific Northwest; the Central American harlequin frog, *Atelopus varius;* and Australia's torrent tree frog, *Litoria nannotis,* have a huge suctorial disc surrounding the mouth—an indicator of their adaptation for life in stream rapids. Using these discs, the tadpoles attach themselves to rocks on the bottom of fast-flowing waters and scrape off algae and other plant growth. Surface-feeding tadpoles of the Malayan horned frog, *Megophrys nasuta,* and the waxy monkey frog, *Phyllomedusa sauvagii,* have large, upwardly positioned funnel mouths. These species live in quiet forest pools, and their big funnel mouths provide a large food-gathering surface.

The African clawed frogs, in *Xenopus* genus, are examples of microphagous tadpoles. They are mid water suspension feeders that hang head down in the water column. With exceptionally large food traps and dense filters, they are the ultimate filtering machines, able to remove prey particles as small as thirteen microns (1 micron = 1/10,000 of a millimeter), an achievement that equals that of the best mechanical sieves designed by man.

Pond tadpoles typically dine on algae and other small particles that grow on submerged surfaces. By contrast, macrophagous tadpoles are adapted to gouging, cutting, and pulverizing. They feed on much larger prey, and some are carnivorous. The strawberry poison frog, *Dendrobates pumilio,* and the granular poison dart frog, *D.*

The tadpole of the American bullfrog

To ensure the survival of the next generation, many frogs lay lots of eggs. If the eggs survive predation, they produce many tadpoles, which also face a multitude of hungry predators (above, an aquatic beetle, *Dysticus marginalis*).

granuliferus, are fed unfertilized eggs laid by attendant females, and tadpoles of the spine-headed tree frog, *Anotheca spinosa,* swallow frog eggs whole. Smokey jungle frog, *Leptodactylus pentadactylus,* tadpoles are notorious predators on other tadpoles, and tadpoles of the *Ceratophrys* genus develop massive jaw muscles and strongly serrated beaks to make quick work of their prey.

The big mouth of the bunch is Budgett's frog, *Lepidobatrachus laevis,* which lives in the Chaco Desert region of Paraguay. It has a big flat head and wide mouth that can suck in tadpoles nearly as large as it is. When the tadpoles of desert-dwelling puddle breeders such as the spadefoot toads, *Scaphiopus,* Mexican burrowing toad, *Rhinophrynus dorsalis,* or African bullfrog, *Pyxicephalus adspersus,* are stressed by drying conditions and vanishing food supplies, they often turn to cannibalism, eating their own kind.

Sensing Prey

Frogs detect and locate food through the fine-tuned use of sight, smell, sound, and the vibrations made by the unwary passing creature. Without question, sight is the most important prey-detecting sense. While some frogs actively chase food items, most are "sit-and-wait" preda-

tors. It is most often movement that triggers their feeding response.

For the goliath frog, *Conraua goliath,* the trigger may be a passing column of army ants or a small bird that makes an error and alights too close. For the barking frog, *Eleutherodactylus augusti,* which frequents limestone caves and rodent burrows in the southwestern United States and Mexico, the feeding response may be stimulated by a camel cricket or a land snail moving about in its retreat. Whatever the kind of movement, it must have the right qualities—size, speed, direction, and manner—before the frog makes the commitment to strike. The southern toad, *Bufo terrestris,* can reject bumblebees by sight alone.

Canny as they are, frogs can make mistakes about what's good to eat and what isn't. They have been known to ingest inanimate objects such as leaves or flowers falling from trees. Dr. James Oliver, a noted herpetologist, once reported that marine toads, *Bufo marinus,* introduced into Hawaii, experienced a fatal seasonal epidemic after feeding on the falling blossoms of the strychnine tree.

Not all feeding is stimulated by movement. Smell, sound, and vibration cues may play roles as well. If biologists feed captive western toads, *Bufo boreas,* a steady diet of crickets and mealworms, the toads will soon begin to tongue-slap spots of odor remaining after the insects are removed. The smell of canned dog food or cat food placed outdoors often attracts toads. The omnivorous marine toad will dine on table scraps of lettuce, avocado, carrot peelings, rice, peas, as well as pet food, dog feces, and rotting vegetation.

Frogs may tune in to the sounds made by their insect prey such as the chirping of crickets.

Large bullfrogs can eat exceptionally large meals. Small birds, mammals, and snakes (like the ribbon snake above) are fair game.

The marine toads and American bullfrogs are attracted by the calls of other frogs, which they will gobble up if they can. Some terrestrial frogs may be stimulated to feed by the subtle vibrations made by passing prey. Aquatic frog species may detect prey using their lateral line system. In the South African clawed frog, *Xenopus muelleri,* that system is made up of conspicuous white dots that look like a line of stitches along the sides of the body. These organs pick up vibrations made by prey moving in the water and help orient the frog toward it, much as the lateral line system functions in fish.

The Big Gulp

Once they've found their food or the food finds them, what happens next looks very uncomfortable for the frog. All carnivorous adult frogs swallow their prey whole. Their teeth are built more for grasping and guiding food, perhaps crushing it, but not for tearing off pieces and chewing. Species that lack teeth often have serrations or

notches along the jaw which aid in grabbing hold of items. So once they have the food in their mouths, frogs generally gulp several times to swallow it. They also retract their eyeballs into the mouth cavity, which helps push the food along to the throat. You'll often see terrestrial frogs wipe their eyes and mouths with their forefeet after they have swallowed a meal, much as humans wipe their mouths with napkins.

Some aquatic species use a gape and suck method of feeding and swallowing. They open their mouths quickly while expanding their throats, causing water to flow in rapidly and bring food with it. They suck out the food, then expel the water back out through their mouths.

Water In and Water Out

About two thirds of the human body is made of water. The same is true of other species, birds, fish, even plants. And it is true of frogs. As much as 80 percent of their body weight may be water. So the organization of water within the cells and tissues has to be very carefully orchestrated. Aquatic species must limit the amount of water their bodies retain, and terrestrial ones must limit the amount of water going out.

As we said earlier, frog skin is highly permeable to water. This is both a benefit and a liability. If the frog's wetland or damp hiding spot dries up, it can lose water rapidly through its skin. However, if water is nearby, the frog can quickly replenish its supply of body water by sitting in it and absorbing the fluid through its skin. Frogs don't actively drink water as reptiles, birds, and mammals do. Instead, they open their mouths and the water soaks through the lining and goes down into the lungs.

On the underside of the pelvic region, true toads and spadefoots have a thin-skinned area called a seat-patch, which comes into contact with the ground when the toads are sitting. Water uptake is especially rapid through this patch, and there is evidence that it also serves a chemical-detecting function. In the red-spotted toad, *Bufo punctatus,* the seat-patch can actually "taste" the quality of the water to be absorbed; water with a high content of salts and urea is avoided.

Studies have shown that amphibians may lose water nearly fifty times faster than a similar-sized lizard, which is protected by its relatively waterproof, scale-covered skin. Some frog species, such as the western spadefoot, *Spea hammondii,* may lose 60 percent of their body water during drought conditions. The degree of dryness of a frog's habitat is an indicator of its tolerance to water loss.

Because their skin is so highly permeable and susceptible to water loss, frogs are always at the mercy of nature. To survive, they depend on a combination of behavioral, structural, and physiological adjustments that have evolved over many millions of years. Behaviorally, most frogs are active at night, thereby limiting their exposure to drying daytime conditions. They may shuttle between a dry feeding site at night and a patch of water during the day. At night, under cool conditions and higher humidity, the marine toad, *Bufo marinus,* often ventures to a feeding site under a porch lamp to eat bugs drawn to the cone of light. Before the heat of the day returns, the toad may hop to a pool of water or a damp shady spot in vegetation some distance away. Similarly, during the day, the green tree frog, *Hyla cinerea,* disappears into a tree pocket or rests quietly on the shady side of a palmetto leaf with its eyes closed, legs tucked tightly to its side, and its body curled to reduce exposure to drying conditions. This tactic is seen in many arboreal frog species around the globe.

Fighting Illness

Frogs, like all life forms, face a host of parasites—fungi, bacteria, and viruses—during their lives. There are uncountable protozoa, intestinal worms, leeches, mites, and ticks (below, marine toad with ticks) that may attack larval and adult amphibians. Herpeslike viruses and others may cause cancer in frogs, and fungi may take advantage of an injury to invade a frog's body. Tadpoles are susceptible to *Candida* and *Saprolegnia,* both parasitic fungi.

When frogs contract infections, they have to depend on their own defensive pharmacy. Faced with bacterial invasion in experimental situations, the edible frog, *Rana esculenta,* moved to a warmer environment and increased its normal preferred body temperature by 8° F. In other words, it ran a fever. By doing so, the frog was able to help its immune system gear up to fight the pathogens.

Some frogs literally use their heads to avoid water loss. The casque-headed tree frogs, *Triprion*, retreat into holes in trees and plug the entrances with their bizarre-shaped bony headgear. Some frogs—like the Australian water-holding frogs, *Cyclorana*, and the Mexican burrowing frog, *Rhinophrynus dorsalis*, are accomplished burrowers

Casque-headed
tree frog,
Triprion spatulatus

and can quickly disappear below the surface when their habitat becomes too hot.

Becoming dormant, or inactive for long periods, is a common tactic used by frogs to escape weather dangerous to them. Some burrowing specialists are able to carry it to extremes. They stay underground without a water refill during prolonged droughts—sometimes for one or more years. When rainstorms finally arrive, they emerge, replenish their body water reserves, and store large amounts of water in their bladders. When needed during their long stay underground, the water diffuses through the bladder wall into the body. For added protection, burrowers like the Australian water-holding frog, the African bullfrog, *Pyxicephalus adspersus*, the Mexican masked tree frog, *Smilisca baudini*, and

the lowland burrowing tree frog, *Pternohyla fodiens*, envelop themselves in layers of shed skin coupled with mucous secretions that harden into a sort of cocoon. The cocoon envelope is a very effective defense mechanism against water loss during long droughts.

Most frogs have a high tolerance for water loss in relation to their body weight. As a group they display remarkable ability to quickly restore their losses. In addition to the physiological adjustments described above, frogs are also able to lower their metabolic rate and metabolize water from their stored fat deposits. Many species produce an antidiuretic hormone called vasotocin. By reducing the secretion and flow of urine, this hormone decreases the tendency to lose water, and it promotes water uptake by the skin from damp soil.

Body Temperature: Getting It Right

Imagine watching a Yosemite toad, *Bufo canorus*, as it tiptoes across a snowfield, with its belly held high, to reach a breeding pool, or an American bullfrog, *Rana catesbeiana*, basking at the edge of a pond on a hot summer day. Rare events in the lives of fragile frogs? Hardly.

Surprisingly, frogs are active over a broad range of temperatures. While few can survive

FROGFACT One way to know how much water loss a frog can tolerate is by looking at where it chooses to live. The desert-dwelling Couch's spadefoot, *Scaphiopus couchii*, is believed to be North America's most water loss–tolerant frog species. It endures dryness better than, for example, the Great Plains toad, *Bufo cognatus* (right), whose prairie grassland home is not as hot and dry as a desert. But the Great Plains toad is much more tolerant of water loss than the mountain yellow-legged frog, *Rana muscosa*, which is found in stream and lakeside habitats of the Sierra Nevadas. As one can imagine, the least tolerant of water loss is the fully aquatic African clawed frog, *Xenopus laevis*, which has been introduced into some southwestern states.

exposure to temperatures higher than 100° F or below 32° F for extended periods, their body temperatures typically range between 37° and 97° F, and average about 81° F. Their temperatures reflect the microhabitats they have chosen to be in at any given time. Frogs from warm climates tolerate high temperatures better than frogs in cooler zones, and conversely, those from cold climates are more cold tolerant than their warm-weather kin.

During a frog's active season it may face periods of high and low temperatures and it actually develops some resistance to these stressful conditions. The ability to acclimate to temperature extremes depends upon the species, its fitness, and the temperatures to which it is exposed. Warm-temperature tolerance may develop in the space of a day as temperature rises or more slowly as seasonal temperatures increase.

Although frogs, like their salamander and caecilian kin, have little internal control over their body temperature, many prefer hot temperatures that are dangerously close to the upper limits they can endure. While they are not as good at it as reptiles, who have developed ways to survive within their very narrow temperature limits, frogs do use behavioral and physiological means to avoid lethal temperatures.

By moving from place to place and changing the position of its body, a frog can take advantage of the best temperatures available to it. Most of the benefits it receives are subtle, but in some cases they are spectacular. On a clear day high in the mountains, an Andean toad, *Bufo spinulosus,* basking in full sunlight in a sheltered spot, is able to increase its body temperature 27° above the air temperature in the shade and reach a body temperature of 90° F. Frogs may change the position of their body for the same purposes. A heat-

By moving around its habitat, a frog can regulate its body temperature. Basking atop a mushroom with much of its skin surface facing the sun (above) allows this frog to increase its temperature to an optimal level for digestion and other functions.

stressed bullfrog sits tall, with its belly off the ground, taking advantage of any cooling breeze. When it is too cool, its body is pressed to the ground.

The speed at which frogs can heat up (or cool down) depends on species, size, age, sunbathing experience, and time of the year. Big frogs gain and lose heat more slowly than small frogs. Dark-colored frogs heat up faster than light-colored ones. Some frogs can dramatically change their colors to take advantage of heating or cooling needs. Frogs at low body temperature can darken the color of the skin so they are capable of increased solar absorption; those at high body temperature can lighten coloration for more solar reflection. Frogs and tadpoles that achieve a preferred body temperature—the temperature zone that suits them best—benefit in many ways. The muscles of hot frogs work better than those of cool frogs of the same species, making them better prepared to catch dinner. Basking frogs that gather in sunny warm-water shallows digest their food much faster than those at lower temperatures. This is a phenomenon of which the frogs seem very much aware. Some basking frogs, like the arboreal green tree frog, *Hyla cinerea,* which can dry out quickly when it is surrounded by dry air, are more conservative in using their supply of body water than nearby terrestrial frogs like the southern leopard frog, *Rana sphenocephala,* that is only a few hops away from a water refill.

Not all frogs and toads bask. Some rarely leave their burrows to come to the surface. Others live in such hot and dry habitats that basking in the sun is not an option, or it is possible only early or late in the day when temperatures are not so fierce. Those frogs that bask regularly are typically active during the day and live in habitats that don't quickly rob them of water.

Some Like It Hot, Some Not

While some frogs like it hot, others prefer to be cool. As a group North and Central American frogs are active from about 37° to 96° F, and their body temperatures average 75° F. Tropical frogs maintain higher body temperatures than their temperate zone cousins. And those living at high altitudes prefer cooler temperatures than frogs living in lowlands. In general if a frog is active on the surface when the air, water, and land about it are warm, it is warm. If the weather is cool, it is cool.

The corroboree frog, *Pseudophryne,* is a cool customer and perhaps one of Australia's most endangered frogs. Corroboree is an Aboriginal word for gathering, or meeting, but it has complex cultural connotations. More than just a physical gathering, it refers to a meeting of minds, a gathering of thoughts, strengths, and dreaming as Aboriginal tribes come together. And a corroboree requires traditional adornments— ocher stripes on dark skin.

For many thousands of years tribes living in the southern highlands gathered for a corroboree on Mount Kosciusko in the summer to feast on bogong moths. At the same time tiny black frogs with vivid yellow stripes gathered for their annual breeding season.

During this time the mountains were alive

The northern corroboree frog, *Pseudophryne pengilleyi,* lives in cool, alpine areas of eastern Australia. Global warming and climate change may have caused temperatures to climb and rainfall to lessen, interfering with the frogs' breeding cycle.

with the males' advertising calls, and over the centuries these tiny frogs and their calls became inextricably linked with the corroboree. Unfortunately, the corroboree frog seems to be fading away, along with the traditional moth hunts.

In the mid-1980s experts noticed that fewer corroboree frogs were gathering during the breeding season. In 1999, 218 frogs were counted in the species' range; in 2004 only 64 were found, a drastic drop. The probable causes of the corroboree's decline are varied and include both human activity and natural environmental changes. Ski resorts and four-wheel-drive vehicles are now found throughout their habitat, destroying the nesting grounds. Climate change and global warming may have made the winters shorter and less cold and caused autumn droughts, disrupting the frogs' breeding cycle and depriving them of the rain they need to flood their nests.

The eastern spadefoot is remarkably adept at digging in sandy soils with its hind feet. It may retreat underground for weeks at a time until rain brings it to the surface.

The corroboree breeds in such a small, specialized area that it is highly vulnerable to physical and environmental stress. In addition, the tadpoles are slow growing and the adults reach sexual maturity later than other frogs. Adults don't breed until they are three to four years old. Unfortunately, by the time scientists figure out why the frog is disappearing, it may already be extinct.

Frozen Frogs Spring to Life!

"I have frequently seen them dug up with the moss, frozen as hard as ice; in which state the legs are easily broken off as a pipestem . . . but by wrapping them in warm skins, and exposing them to a slow fire, they soon recover life." These are the words found in the journal of Samuel Hearne, who journeyed in the Arctic from 1769 to 1772. Could they be true?

Hearne was not alone with his frozen frog tales. Similar reports appeared in the logbooks of other eighteenth-century European explorers who visited the icy frontiers of North America. For two hundred years these stories were largely dismissed as tall tales. It wasn't until 1982 that scientists began looking closely at the ability of frogs to survive subzero temperatures.

The wood frog, *Rana sylvatica,* ranges farther north than any other North American amphibian or reptile. At the north end of its distribution it may be seen from Labrador, across Canada, to Alaska. How does this frog—which hibernates on land, near the surface, under forest litter, mats of vegetation, or rocks—survive subzero temperature levels?

The wood frog belongs to a short, but growing, list of fish, amphibians, reptiles, and invertebrates that have been discovered to be freeze-tolerant.

Several species of frogs in North America and one in Europe can survive subzero temperatures during the winter. High concentrations of glucose in the body act as antifreeze, protecting sensitive tissues as the water in the body turns to ice.

As winter approaches and temperatures fall below freezing, the wood frog's heart rate and breathing slow to a halt, its eyes become cloudy, and its body grows stiff. As much as 65 percent of the water in the spaces between cells in its tissues may gradually crystallize into ice. Rapid freezing is lethal for all animals, but slow cooling is another story. The wood frog is able to withstand temperatures as low as 20° F during slow cooling over a period of several hours. This is possible because it is able to saturate its body with glucose, a sugar. During the cooling process, glucose concentrations in the frog's central organs may soar to a hundred times their original levels by means of a very dramatic breakdown of the glycogen stored in the liver. The high concentration of

FROGFACT Frogs that are able to survive the deep-freeze winter conditions of the Far North are now being recognized for their potential contributions to human medicine. Scientists are looking at freeze-tolerant frogs and the mechanisms that keep their tissues alive under frigid conditions as they explore ways to develop techniques to freeze and maintain vital human organs so they can later be transplanted into people who need them desperately.

North America's wood frog, *Rana sylvatica* (left), is extremely tolerant of cold temperatures and is one of the first amphibians to emerge from winter hibernation.

these harsh environments may be a natural progression from their ability to withstand severe dehydration.

Freeze-tolerant frogs were initially thought to be a New World phenomenon, but recently the European common frog, *Rana temporaria,* has been shown to be able to enter and leave the frozen state without harm. No doubt the list will grow as biologists continue to explore the survival strategies of frogs that live at the edges of animal tolerances.

glucose acts as an antifreeze, lowering the body's freezing point to protect the sensitive tissues, while the remaining water in the body turns to ice.

The wood frog does little to prepare itself for the deep freeze, but studies have shown that as winter approaches, it begins to store glycogen in the liver. Concentrations may reach two- to tenfold the level found in frogs that hibernate in ponds. When warm weather returns, the wood frog's organs with the highest levels of glucose—heart, liver, and kidneys—thaw first and allow normal metabolic activity to return.

In North America the wood frog, the spring peeper, *Pseudacris crucifer,* the chorus frog, *P. triseriata,* and the gray tree frog, *Hyla versicolor,* share the ability to survive in subzero conditions over winter. Biologists believe that freeze tolerance among these amphibian explorers of the cold northlands evolved very recently, when the last Ice Age drew to a close some 13,000 to 20,000 years ago. As the enormous ice sheets retreated northward, the frogs extended their ranges into the newly exposed landscape. The freeze tolerance that allowed the frogs to occupy

The gray tree frog, *Hyla versicolor,* also is freeze-tolerant (above, in frozen state). As the outside temperature starts to warm in the spring, the organs with the most glucose—the heart, liver, and kidneys—begin to thaw and the frog slowly returns to normal (left).

CHAPTER FOUR

CATCH ME IF YOU CAN

IF WE HUMANS think it is a tough world out there, imagine what it is like for frogs. For them, staying alive is a full-time job. Frogs are not equipped with a tough coat of armor, claws, fangs, or a cutting beak like some of the creatures that evolved after them. Rather, they are small, soft-skinned, and at the mercy of legions of predators, right from the first spark of life. As a result, only a small percentage survive to reproduce.

Frogs, however, have evolved a host of adaptations to avoid and fool the predators who would do them harm. One of the simplest ways they defend themselves against predation is by producing an enormous number of eggs. The female marine toad, *Bufo marinus,* can lay as many as 30,000 eggs in one clutch. Even tiny species, like Australia's corroboree frog, *Pseudophryne corroboree,* which measures about an inch, lay upward of thirty eggs at a time.

There are other ways frogs seem to have "learned" to protect themselves. In some species the adults are programmed to an early breeding season. The wood frog, *Rana sylvatica,* breeds mainly in the early spring, before many of its predators emerge from hibernation. Scientists

have discovered that in the southern leopard frog, *Rana sphenocephala,* eggs that are laid in water inhabited by crawfish hatch significantly faster than eggs laid in ponds without predatory crawfish. The embryos of the red-eyed tree frog, *Agalychnis callidryas,* will often hatch early to escape from snakes, wasps, and pathogenic fungus.

Of course these strategies are not nearly enough to ensure survival. There are many predators that like to eat frog eggs and will scarf them up whenever and wherever they can. Frog eggs laid in water are a favorite food item of aquatic invertebrates, fish, salamanders, and turtles. On land, beetles, snakes, and birds will happily dine on any frog eggs they can find. During the frog breeding season in

Frogs and toads spend their entire lives trying to avoid being eaten by other animals. They have evolved a host of adaptations and behaviors to deter raccoons (left), crocodiles (above), and other predators.

the Ivory Coast of Africa, the Diana monkey and the sooty mangabey (another type of monkey) search trees and rocks on the edges of ponds for the nests of an Old World foam-nest tree frog, *Chiromantis rufescens.* They're also fond of the jellylike egg masses of sedge frogs, *Hyperolius,* which are stuck to leaves above the water. When the monkeys discover this frog caviar, they scoop the foam and eggs out of the nest and eat them with enthusiasm. Even the egg masses of tropical American tree frogs, laid on leaves high in a tree above water, are not safe. The cat-eyed snake, *Leptodeira septentrionalis,* specializes in finding and devouring these eggs. It surrounds the end of an egg mass with its jaws and works them forward to encompass the entire clutch.

Even after aquatic tadpoles hatch and break free of their egg coats, they do not leave trouble behind. Many of these same aquatic predators await them. Predacious diving beetles, giant water bugs, water scorpions, and dragonfly larvae are quick to seize the tadpoles and suck the life out of them. Other amphibians sharing the pond— especially in temporary pools—are major predators. In the eastern United States, the newt, *Notophthalmus viridescens,* the larvae of the tiger salamander, *Ambystoma tigrinum,* and marbled salamanders, *A. opacum,* take their share. Along wetland edges snakes such as the common garter, *Thamnophis sirtalis,* the ribbon, *T. sauritus,* and the northern water snake, *Nerodia sipedon,* as well as raccoons, skunks, opossums, herons, and egrets all forage for tadpoles and for metamorphosing and adult frogs.

It would almost be easier to list the animals that don't eat frogs than those that do. Tarantulas and hunting spiders jump on small frogs and inject them with their venoms. Freshwater crabs grab them at the edges of streams and have a feast. While most snakes that eat frogs aren't that fussy about which ones they consume, some are specialists. The African green snake, *Philothamus,* appears to prefer sedge frogs, while the eastern hog-nosed snake, *Heterodon platirhinos,* and the

FROGFACT Among the many mammal species that prey on frogs, there are both an Old and a New World species of bat that have learned to zero in on calling frogs and grab them.

African night adder, *Causus rhombiatus,* limit their menu to true toads in the genus *Bufo.* South American false vipers, *Xenodon,* have similar feeding habits but also like wide-bodied frogs such as the smokey jungle frog, *Leptodactylus pentadactylus.* Some large carnivorous bullfrogs have gluttonous appetites for smaller frogs. And of course crocodiles and alligators, aquatic turtles, and predatory fish will make quick work of frogs that venture too close.

The few frogs that survive the onslaught of predators have run a gauntlet of diseases, predators, and environmental perils. Is it survival of the fittest or extreme good luck that help them live? No doubt, survival of the fittest plays a role, but survivors also enjoy a very large dose of good fortune. Good luck for a frog means starting life in a pond or stream that doesn't dry up, finding plenty of food in its habitat, and encountering few pathogens, parasites, and predators. On the rare occasion when this happens, it is a good year for frogs. In addition to luck, survival requires some highly tuned physical attributes and the successful deployment of a battery of defenses.

This gray tree frog hides from predators by resting quietly on a tree trunk, where its skin color and pattern blend in with the lichens.

Hide-and-Seek

One favorite survival technique of frogs might be called hide-and-seek. And just as in the childhood game, remaining motionless so as not to catch the eye of a predator is a key to winning. Add a measure or two of camouflage, and the odds of not being eaten increase. It's not surprising that many frogs and toads are green, gray, or brown, with mottled markings or patterns that blend well with their surroundings. The gray tree frog, *Hyla versicolor,* often rests silently on the side of a tree, its bark-colored skin and lichenlike patterns blending perfectly with the tree trunk. The tan-and-brown Malayan horned frog, *Megophrys nasuta*

adds cryptic body structures to its basic camouflage strategy. This frog is amazingly well camouflaged. Peaks of bone and skin over its eyes and scalloped folds of skin on its legs look like leaf edges and break up the frog's outline. They are very difficult to spot among the dead leaves of their forest floor habitat.

The American toad may sit very still in a crouched position when a garter snake approaches. If touched by the snake's body, the toad doesn't move. But if it is touched by the snake's head, near the dangerous mouth, the toad hops away, breaking up its chemical trail to avoid detection, and crouches again.

The "horns" over the eyes of this Asian leaf frog, *Megophrys nasuta* (above), and its coloring make it difficult to see among the real leaves of the forest floor.

The Long Jump

Many of the frogs with which we are most familiar use the "long jump" tactic of escape. Walk along the edge of a pond, and you will probably see frogs make single bounds from land to water and disappear. It is the basic escape plan of many ranid frogs, such as North America's green frog, *Rana clamitans,* and the foothill yellow-bellied frog, *R. boylii.* In West Africa, the enormous goliath frog, *Conraua goliath,* also uses a single-jump escape strategy. Because of its size, it tires quickly, and if forced to take several jumps it becomes exhausted. So the goliath frog is never far from the river's edge, where a single bound will carry it to safety.

> **FROGFACT** With their long legs, many species of frogs can leap twenty times the length of their bodies.

Jumping is the basic escape plan for many frogs, like this North American green frog.

However, a number of frogs have relatively short legs and are not good jumpers. So when they're disturbed, they make a series of straightaway jumps, or they might move in a zigzag pattern of short leaps, after which they remain motionless. The Australian rocket frog, *Litoria nasuta,* is a long jumper but often makes a quick series of long leaps to break its scent trail and distance itself from its pursuer. Tree frogs often leap from one branch to another, which makes it impossible for many predators to follow them. And Wallace's flying frog, *Rhacophorus nigropalmatus,* and its close kin may make the extreme survivor move, launching themselves from the tree canopy and gliding to safety in another tree. They spread their legs and use the enormous webbing between their fingers and toes as parachutes, allowing them a safe landing— usually.

Frogs may display brilliant warning colors on their backs or have a rainbow of "flash colors" on their flanks and legs. Some, like this Perez's snouted frog, *Edalorhina perezi*, have camouflaged colors on their backs and startling colors on their bellies.

Warning, Danger Ahead

Bright red, orange, or yellow colors—especially when set against a dark background—signal danger. As a child, you may have heard the ditty that warns of the difference between the venomous coral snake and its mimic, the harmless tricolor king snake. "Red against black is a friend of Jack, red touching yellow can kill a fella." Make a mistake, and the results might be deadly.

Like the coral snake, many brightly colored frogs can be very dangerous. When challenged, the somber-colored fire-bellied

The bright belly of the mildly toxic Oriental fire-bellied toad, *Bombina orientalis*, warns some—but not all—predators away. This toad is very common in shallow waters in villages and local agriculture fields.

toads, *Bombina,* assume what is called the "unken reflex," a swaybacked position with their head and rump elevated to expose the fiery red, orange, or yellow warning colors of their undersides. This defensive position signals predators that they are toxic.

All frogs and toads produce protective mucus and toxins in their skin. True toads also possess a greatly enlarged pair of parotoid glands, located behind their head, which have a high concentra-

tion of toxins. Toads will tilt their bodies forward and present their parotoid glands in readiness to deliver the toxins. The largest member of the family, the cane toad, *Bufo marinus,* is quite adept at this and, when its parotoid glands are compressed, can squirt its poisons into the mouth or eyes of an attacker three feet away. The South American false-eyed frog, *Physalaemus nattereri,* exposes its elevated rump, which has two enormous eyelike spots that are armed and ready to deliver an unpleasant substance—a shocking display indeed.

For the most part, the toxins produced by

frogs are relatively harmless to the predators that feed on them. Some frogs, however, produce some of the deadliest natural toxins known. Many hundreds of frog toxins—alkaloids—have been identified. The most potent of them belong to the "living jewels," the enamel-like poison frogs, which are bathed in warning colors and patterns. Always ready to serve a cocktail of poisons, the strawberry, *Dendrobates pumilio,* golden, *Phyllobates terribilis,* and harlequin poison frog, *Dendrobates histrionicus,* poison frogs and their strikingly colored relatives openly forage in the forest for minute prey during the day, undaunted by snakes, birds, rodents, and other frog predators. If a predator makes a mistake and bites a poison frog, it is usually its last mistake.

Some totally harmless species mimic the colors of the poison frogs. This deceptive coloration may spare the mimics from predators that have learned to associate certain colors with noxious taste and incapacitation. The palatable Fort Randolph robber frog, *Eleutherodactylus gaigeae,* mimics the highly toxic poison frog, *Phyllobates*

You Are What You Eat

Scientists have been searching for the source of frog toxins for more than thirty years. Early on, they found out that strawberry poison frogs, *Dendrobates pumilio,* kept in the laboratory lost their toxicity when fed diets of tiny crickets and fruit flies. The frogs couldn't seem to manufacture their toxins in captivity. Led by Dr. John Daly, a pioneer in frog toxins, the search was launched for their source in the wild. His colleagues collected and analyzed five hundred samples of small arthropods from sites where poison frogs are found. Mystery solved: ants! The crucial ant samples were collected from Heliconia plants during the rainy season, when poison frogs were raising their tadpoles in the water pools at the leaf bases. The same ant species containing the toxins were found in the stomach contents of strawberry poison frogs. Now the search is on for the ant's dietary source of the toxins.

The brilliant warning colors of the poison frogs signal to predators that they are toxic and very dangerous to eat. The golden poison frog, *Phyllobates terribilis* (left and opposite page right), has enough batrachotoxin to kill 20,000 mice and is unsafe for humans to handle. The imitator frog, *Dendrobates imitator* (opposite page far left), looks like several other poison frog species, which reinforces its own toxic status to predators.

Below, the harlequin poison frog, *D. histrionicus*, displays a wide variety of color combinations. No two individuals look exactly alike.

lugubris. Another frog, the aptly named *Dendrobates imitator,* is, in fact, poisonous and looks almost identical to several other poison frogs that share its range. This is referred to as Müllerian mimicry, which occurs when two toxic species mimic one another's warning colors. To the predator it more fully broadcasts the colors and patterns to avoid. It is thought to be a safety in numbers mechanism that reduces losses from predators that haven't yet learned their lessons.

Some frogs "play possum." By closing its eyes, making its body go limp, or flopping over on its back and lying still, it can fool a predator into believing that it's already dead or unappealing.

Playing Dead and Other Ploys

So what's a frog to do when its basic escape plan fails? It may play dead, puff up to look bigger, assume bizarre positions to confuse its attacker, display warning colors to intimidate the opposition, scream, or fight back.

Sometimes amphibians are caught off guard when suddenly threatened, and they need a moment to reorganize. A frog playing possum, with eyes closed and body limp or contorted as if injured or dead, is an unappealing picture to a predator looking for a fresh meal. Its "search image" for appropriate prey may be thrown off when the morsel before it just doesn't look right. To fool a predator, the Mexican tree frog, *Pachymedusa dacnicolor,* tucks its legs to its sides and lies motionless on its back. Other frogs extend and stiffen their legs in unnatural positions and remain still. The smokey jungle frog

and its close relatives may inflate their lungs, dramatically increasing their size, which may startle the aggressor and change its perception of the meal: The frog may look too big to swallow.

During the day the red-eyed tree frog, *Agalychnis callidryas,* sits on leaves with its bright green body well camouflaged against the background. Its eyes are closed, and its legs are tucked in tight against its sides. When disturbed, the tree frog will pop open its large enamel-like red eyes. If that doesn't drive the harasser away, the frog may further intimidate with a display of "flash colors"—the rainbow of bright colors along the frog's belly when it starts to move. The total effect is stunning, and any hesitancy by the disoriented predator will give the frog an opportunity to escape.

Red-eyed tree frog,
Agalychnis callidryas

Banshees and Biters

When their life is on the line and frogs are grabbed or suddenly overwhelmed by a predator, it is time for drastic action. Many a herpetologist has been startled by the sudden scream of a frog he or she has captured. This vocalization is known as the distress call. One of the most impressive distress calls belongs to the smokey jungle frog. When grabbed or picked up, it screams like the proverbial scalded cat, and one's first reaction is to drop it.

Unlike the male frogs' familiar advertisement call, which is made with the mouth closed, the distress call is explosive, often loud, and made with the mouth wide open. Distress calls are not made to warn other frogs of danger, but to startle the attacker.

Some frogs turn up the volume. White's tree frog, *Litoria caerulea,* often retires to tree hollows during Australia's dry season and is known for its piercing screams when disturbed by monitor lizards that have designs on the same retreat.

The distress call may be accompanied by other startling behaviors. One of the marsupial frogs makes a series of long buzzing-like noises and displays its bluish green tongue and mouth cavity. And the Australian water-holding frog seems to be able to forecast a predator's action and screams in anticipation of being grabbed. It opens its mouth, jumps straight up into the air, and falls to the ground where it had been resting.

The ultimate defense is biting. African bullfrogs and South American horned frogs, with their large heads and strong jaws, are quick to bite aggressors. These are favorite species of frog hobbyists, and many of them have been bloodied when their fingers passed too close to the jaws of one of these "pets."

Australian brown tree frog, *Litoria ewingi*

Stinkpots

Some frogs stink. The mink frog, *Rana septentrionalis,* of northeastern North America smells like its musky mammal namesake. People also find the odors of South America's waxy monkey frogs, *Phyllomedusa,* and the European common spadefoot, *Pelobates fuscus,* objectionable. Are predators fazed by these frog smells? Maybe. The Australian brown tree frog, *Litoria ewingi,* produces a powerful odor. Biologists have discovered that its stench repels biting flies and is a strong deterrent to predation by the water python, *Liasis fuscus.* Where does the smell come from? The obnoxious chemicals come from plants in the frog's environment. It appears that frogs absorb these bug and snake retardants through their skin while sitting on the plants and eating prey that have fed on the plants.

Mink frog,
Rana septentrionalis

FROG FAMILIES

CHAPTER FIVE
FROG FAMILIES

HOW MANY FROG SPECIES are there in the world? Six thousand? Ten thousand? The simple answer is that nobody knows. As of March 2005 the AmphibiaWeb database contained the scientific names of 5069 frogs and toads that have been officially recognized. That's about 35 percent more than were recognized in 1985, and that figure will almost certainly grow during the next few decades. The number of species tends to increase in fits and starts, as amphibian specialists set their research sights on parts of the world that are known as biodiversity hot spots and that have not been fully explored for new frogs.

Hot Spots for Frogs

Biodiversity hot spots are areas that have especially large numbers of plant and animal species. The American tropics are a prime example. More than 40 percent of the world's identified frogs are from this region. Ecuador, which is on the Pacific Ocean at the equator, has 425 known amphibians—the largest number of amphibians per unit of area on earth. And it recently became one species richer. The newest addition is the Tapichalacan tree frog, *Hyla tapichalaca,* which was discovered by a team of Ecuadorian and America herpetologists along a small, cascading stream in montane cloud forest. This tree frog is large—about two and one-half inches in length—and quite colorful, with a pale blue body and white-tipped fingers and toes.

Why was this colorful living jewel discovered only recently? Its habitat has been difficult to reach, and scientists have just lately begun surveying the region for wildlife. This remote area of South America will likely yield more new frogs in the years to come.

Large islands such as Madagascar, New Guinea, and Borneo are also frog hot spots. Scores of new frogs have been found there in recent years, and more await discovery. One startling new hot spot

Earth's tropical regions are full of frogs, ranging from the Argentine horned toad (pages 70–71), to the Cameroon big-eyed tree frog (opposite), to one of the world's newest discoveries, the white-tipped Tapichalacan tree frog, *Hyla tapichalaca,* from Ecuador (above).

FROGFACT When a potential predator annoys a Tapichalacan tree frog, the frog's skin secretes a sticky, stinky white fluid. The frog also gives a dramatic warning display by spreading out its rear legs and tucking its head between its front legs, which it places under its chin. The frog holds its rump high and its head low, exposing distinctive white patches on its elbows, heels, and vent area.

that has amazed frog biologists and biodiversity specialists is Sri Lanka, an island in the Indian Ocean south of India. Rohan Pethiyagoda, a biomedical engineer who founded the Wildlife Heritage Trust of Sri Lanka, is waging a personal crusade to save what remains of his nation's rich natural heritage. Before 1987 scientists believed there were about thirty-six species of frogs on Sri Lanka, and the island was not expected to yield significant numbers of new frogs. Then the trust arranged to survey the nation's few patches of rain forest. Even though much of the island was cleared during the British colonial period to create tea, coffee, and rubber plantations, and less than 2 percent of Sri Lanka's original rain forest cover remains, Pethiyagoda and his team collected more than a thousand frog specimens at three hundred sites. They soon discovered that they had found an astonishing number of new frogs—more than a hundred new species that run the gamut from large, colorful tree dwellers to tiny leaf-litter inhabitants. The discovery makes Sri Lanka a new center of frog biodiversity and increases the urgency to protect its precious rain forest. It also sends another signal that we know very little about biodiversity and cannot presume to know what places will be rich in wildlife.

New species are also being added when scientists reexamine groups that have been identified as one species. Usually there are clues that more than one species may be "buried" in what was

FROGFACT Sadly, just as scientists are finding new frogs, some species are vanishing, victims of hostile man-made or natural conditions. The World Conservation Union (IUCN) uses the following stages to rank just how imperiled an organism is. From the minimal to the worst, they are: Least Concern, Near Threatened, Vulnerable, Endangered, Critically Endangered, and Extinct.

thought to be a single species. The difference may be in the structure of the vocalizations the frogs make. Or it may be that two populations of what had been identified as one frog species have very different lifestyles or behaviors. Research into these differences, as well as an examination of physical traits and DNA variations, may reveal that more than one species is represented. North America's northern leopard frog, *Rana pipiens,* is a good example.

In 1782 H. Schreber described a frog he discovered in New York State as the leopard frog and gave it the scientific name *Rana pipiens.* For over two hundred years that name was used for all leopard frogs from Washington to Maine, California to Florida, and Canada to Panama. Recently, however, frog specialists discovered that there are at least twenty different species of leopard frogs in what they call the *R. pipiens* species complex. They are still working on this complex, and it is very likely that more species will be added as taxonomists improve their identification tools.

The odds of finding new frogs improve as you head toward the equator, because most thrive in warm, humid environments and avoid the extreme frozen parts of the world. Frogs are not

Sri Lanka, in the Indian Ocean, is a center of frog diversity (far right, Shrub frog, *Philautus femoralis*). In the 1990s Rohan Pethiyagoda (near right) and his team discovered more than a hundred new species there.

found in Antarctica, as noted earlier, or in Greenland and the arctic lands of the Far North. Frogs are also rarely found on remote oceanic islands that are volcanic or coral in origin. These spots are simply too far out in the salty seas for frogs to reach them by floating on vegetation. If frogs do turn up on these islands, they most likely have been introduced by people. Fiji in the South Pacific and the Seychelles off the east coast of Africa are exceptions. They have a few frog species that occur nowhere else. It is presumed that in some distant past these islands were connected to, or perhaps were close to, large landmasses and that the frogs drifted with the islands as they separated from the mainland.

The chances of finding new frog species are best in the unexplored areas of the tropics. The high canopies of rain forests, for example, are proving to have treasure troves of new animal and plant species, including frogs. In addition, innovative sampling techniques are helping biologists find both cryptic frogs that live at the top of the green world as well as species that spend nearly all of their lives underground.

Classifying Frogs: A Tricky Business

The business of naming living things, taxonomy, has been a hotbed of controversy since its earliest days. Frog experts are no different from specialists in other fields; they have always debated the taxonomic relationships of the animals they study. Specialists continually reorganize the families,

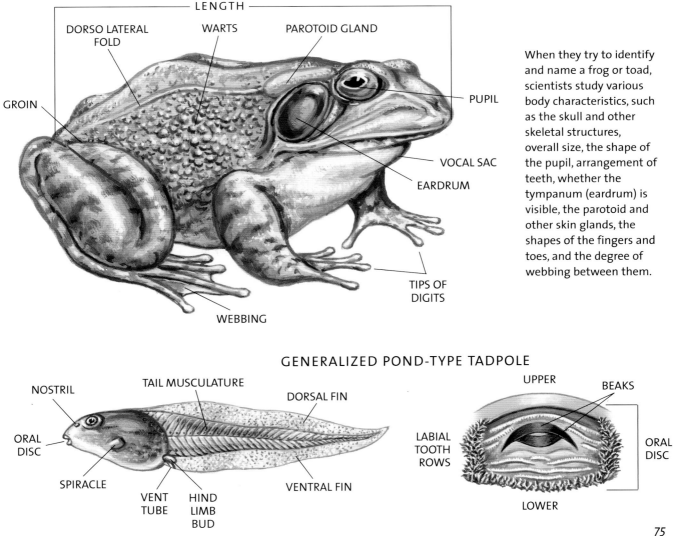

When they try to identify and name a frog or toad, scientists study various body characteristics, such as the skull and other skeletal structures, overall size, the shape of the pupil, arrangement of teeth, whether the tympanum (eardrum) is visible, the parotoid and other skin glands, the shapes of the fingers and toes, and the degree of webbing between them.

GENERALIZED POND-TYPE TADPOLE

and the groups of genera within them, as new information becomes available.

Defining frog families using traditional characteristics seems to be an impossible task. To make their decision as to which family they assign a specimen, biologists closely examine features of the skull, the vertebrae, the pectoral and pelvic girdles, elements of the toes, and the limb muscles. They also use the type of amplexus and the body design of the tadpole. Molecular studies also provide relationship clues. Yet many frog families have not been well defined, and controversy is likely to continue for a very long time. There are many missing parts to the riddle of frog relation-

FROGFACT Where do the Latin names come from? The species name is often based upon a distinctive feature, behavioral trait, or place of origin, or is meant to honor the discoverer or some other person. For example, the bird-voiced tree frog is known scientifically as *Hyla avivoca*. *Hyla* is a genus in the tree frog family. The species name refers to its distinctive call. It's derived from the Latin for bird (*avis*) and voice (*vocalis*). *Hyla tapichalaca* was named for the Tapichalaca caldera where it was discovered, and *Hyla berthalutzae* was named in honor of Bertha Lutz for her extensive studies of Brazilian frogs.

ships, and perhaps it will never be settled once and for all. In recent times, for example, the brightly colored, toxic mantella frogs of Madagascar have been considered to be most closely related to the true frogs in the family Ranidae. However, some experts believed that

The Purple Burrowing Frog Makes It Thirty

Frog men and women are thrilled! A new, bright purple, bloated, short-legged, tiny-eyed frog with a very unusual pointy snout built for burrowing was discovered in 2003 in southern India by Franky Bossuyt and S. D. Biju of the Free University of Brussels in Belgium. While many new frogs are found each year, this purple frog, genus *Nasikabatrachus* species *sahyadrensis*, is very special. In Sanskrit, *Nasika* means nose, *Batrachus* means frog, and *Sahyadri* refers to the Western Ghats, the low-lying mountains along India's west coast, where the frog was found. Based on DNA analysis, this is not just a new species, but a whole new family—Nasikabatrachidae. So far, it's a family of only one, and one that hopped about at the feet of the dinosaurs.

The purple frog's discovery has been described as a once-in-a-century find. The last new frog family was discovered nearly eighty years earlier. The closest relatives of *Nasikabatrachus* are the Seychelles frogs (Family Sooglossidae), which live eighteen hundred miles away. *Nasikabatrachus* apparently separated from this family about 130 million years ago during the heyday of the dinosaurs, before the Seychelles Islands broke away from the Indian subcontinent some 65 million years ago.

they belong in the Afro-Asian tree frog family Rhacophoridae. There are other specialists who believe that the mantellas and their close kin warrant a family of their own, the Mantellidae.

So, depending upon the herpetological authority you follow, the current number of generally recognized frog families is twenty-eight or twenty-nine . . . or is it thirty? We have chosen to go with the very latest available information and cover thirty families.

To complicate things further, frog specialists group these families into suborders—the Archaeobatrachians, which they believe are the most primitive frogs, with nine families and two hundred species; and the Neobatrachians, considered to be the more advanced frogs, which has more than 4750 species. For ease of location, the frog families that follow are simply placed in alphabetical order by their scientific names, followed by their common names.

Ruthven's frog,
Allophryne ruthveni

Family Allophrynidae
Ruthven's Frog

This entire family consists of one species, Ruthven's frog, *Allophryne ruthveni*, which is a rather confusing creature. Since its discovery in 1926 in what is now Guyana, scientists have moved it from one family to another and then another: from the true toads into the southern frogs and then to the glass and tree frogs. However, it doesn't seem to fit the definitions of any of the other frog families, so

finally it was given its own.

This tiny frog, about one inch in length, lives in the trees of the rain forests found in Venezuela, Guyana, French Guiana, Suriname, and Brazil. It is slender and flat-headed with a round snout, long legs, and long toes that are equipped with flat-ended toe pads. Both the males and females range in color from bronze or gold to yellowish tan and have golden-yellow back

stripes. During breeding, males gather around pools at the beginning of the rainy season, when hundreds of them may be heard chorusing at night after storms, wooing the females. After the male clasps her in amplexus—the breeding embrace—the female lays several hundred eggs on leaves above pools. The tadpoles hatch, drop into the water, and develop there.

Hairy frog, *Trichobatrachus robustus*

Family Arthroleptidae
Squeaker Frogs

This small family has about eighty species of frogs that are found across Africa below the Sahara. The family gets its common name from the distinctive voices of its members. They are also called screechers, and their calls sound something like the calls of crickets.

Many squeakers are about one to one and one-half inches in length, and colored like the leaf litter of the rain forest floor where they live. Squeakers appear to be closely related to the Ranidae family, the true frogs, and are sometimes grouped with them. Many have very broad heads, slender bodies, and long legs—just what we think of when we think of frogs.

Male squeakers call to females from elevated sites on shrub branches or in hollow trees. Females lay two or three clutches of large eggs in small cavities on land at various times during the reproductive season. The young develop directly in the egg and hatch as tiny froglets. This species has a very short life span—less than a year.

The hairy frog, *Trichobatrachus robustus,* found in some parts of Africa, is the most bizarre member of this family. It is actually unique among frogs. It reaches a length of more than four inches and has an unusual head—large in proportion to the frog's body and broader than it is long. The snout is short and rounded, and the nostrils are positioned closer to the eyes than to the tip of the snout.

Male hairy frogs are much bigger than the females, and they develop long, shaggy, hair-like structures on their flanks and thighs during the breeding season. This frog has small lungs, so it is believed that the hairy projections, which are richly supplied with tiny blood vessels, assist the male with breathing, allowing it to stay underwater longer. It has been reported that after the female lays her eggs on rocks on the stream bottom, the male sits in attendance on top of them.

Family Ascaphidae
Tailed Frogs

Tailed frogs live in the cold, clean, swift-moving, cobble-bottomed streams of the Pacific Northwest. There are two species. The coastal tailed frog, *Ascaphus truei*, ranges along the Pacific coast from northern California to British Columbia and has been found from sea level to timberline. In 2001, using DNA evidence, researchers discovered that the inland population of tailed frogs isolated in northern Idaho and western Montana had separated at some point into a different species, *Ascaphus montanus*.

Tailed frogs are considered to be among the most ancient frogs living today. It's their "tail" that distinguishes them from all other frogs. This unique structure, seen only in the adult males, is actually an extension of

Tailed frog, *Ascaphus montanus*

the cloaca, a sort of pouch in the frog's hind area that is associated with reproduction, among other things. This extension allows the male to fertilize the female internally, so the sperm don't wash away in the torrential waters of the frog's habitat.

Tailed frogs are about two inches long and reddish brown to gray in color. They have a black line running from the tip of the snout through the eye to the shoulder. They lack a tympanum and are believed to be deaf, probably an evolutionary accom-

modation because the streams in which they live are so noisy they wouldn't be able to hear one another call.

Tailed frogs are shy creatures, seldom seen. They are most active at night and may venture only a short distance from their stream in search of insects. Mating occurs in the early fall. The following summer the female attaches fifty to sixty pea-sized eggs in strings under a rock in the stream. The tadpoles have very large, round, sucker-like mouths with which they attach themselves to the undersides of rocks and debris in the stream to avoid being swept away in the current. They have been seen using their oral discs to help them climb from rock to rock out of streams into the spray zone. Giant salamanders, *Dicamptodon,* share the same habitat and are fierce predators, consuming lots of tadpoles. Tailed frogs can survive predation, but they cannot tolerate the sedimentation and water temperature changes in their habitat that accompany clearcut timbering and road construction near their streams.

The Frog Kick

Ancient frogs may have jumped as their descendants do today, but they probably didn't swim the same way nearly all modern frogs do. The evidence for this can be found in two of the primitive families, the tailed (Ascaphidae) and the New Zealand frogs (Leiopelmatidae). When these frogs jump, they leap like other frogs, kicking their hind legs symmetrically and at the same time. Most frogs swim in much the same way: with their front legs held back against their sides to reduce drag, their hind legs acting as thrusters, and their feet as paddles. When the tailed and New Zealand frogs swim, their front legs are stretched out forward, and they propel themselves with alternating movements of their hind legs. The hind leg that is outstretched acts like a rudder. Their movements are not unlike those of tadpoles, with their bodies swaying from side to side. Nevertheless, they are able to swim a steady course, and perhaps they provide a glimpse into the way frogs swam in the distant past.

Family Bombinatoridae
Fire-Bellied Toads

The family consists of eleven small to medium-sized, semi-aquatic toads whose brightly colored bellies advertise their warning. They are mildly toxic and a display of their underside stops some predators—but not all. Their bodies are flattened, their skins are warty, and their eyes have an unusual triangular-shaped pupil.

"Bombinas" are bold and adaptive. They are active during the day and live in the stagnant ditches, puddles, ponds, swamps, and stream backwaters in a variety of landscapes. The oriental fire-bellied toad, *B. orientalis,* is found at 5300–10,000 feet above sea level in southeastern Siberia, northeastern China, and Korea. This species has a long breeding season, with females laying eggs at different times until the supply is exhausted. The sizes of the egg clutches range from about forty to two hundred and fifty eggs. The egg and tadpole stages last about two months, and transformation takes place in late summer. *B. orientalis* are quite hardy and live as long as twenty years.

The European fire-bellied toad, *B. bombina,* of central and eastern Europe, has a similar life history and is abundant in some areas of its range. Drainage canals have served as pathways for it to disperse. Unfortunately, this species has disappeared from some regions because of habitat destruction and pollution.

The remaining two species in the family are the larger, and less colorful, flat-headed frogs, *Barbourula busuangensis* and *B. kalimantenensis,* from the southern Philippines and northern Borneo, respectively. The Philippine flat-headed frog is highly aquatic and lives in fast-moving mountain streams in undisturbed forests. Its fingers and toes have extensive webbing, an adaptation to its lifestyle. It is active in low light and is very wary, but can be spotted floating at the water's surface with only its eyes and nostrils exposed. However, when disturbed it is quick to depart to its underwater hideouts.

Oriental fire-bellied toad, *Bombina orientalis*

Gold frog, *Brachycephalus ephippium*

Family Brachycephalidae
Three-Toed Toadlets

This is a family of midgets! While there is debate as to whether there are two or six species in the family, no one disagrees that these are among the tiniest frogs. The flea frog, *Psyllophryne didactyla,* is less than half an inch in length, and the bright orange–colored gold frog, *Brachycephalus ephippium,* rarely reaches two thirds of an inch. Family members have only three toes on each foot and two fingers on each hand. They are terrestrial, inhabiting the damp leaf litter on the floors of the Atlantic forests of southeastern Brazil. Gold frogs produce small clutches of eggs that they coat with soil particles, which may serve as camouflage and help protect the eggs from drying out. The eggs undergo direct development, and the young hatch as very, very small replicas of the adults.

Flea frog, *Psyllophryne didactyla*

Family Bufonidae
True Toads

Just as true frogs exemplify frogs, true toads are the epitome of what toads should look like—squat-bodied, with short legs and rather drab-colored warty skin. This large family has thirty-three genera and more than four hundred and fifty species. More than half of the species are in the genus *Bufo*, a diverse group. *Bufo* ranges in size from the elfin one-inch oak toad, *Bufo quercicus*, found in the Coastal Plains of the southeastern United States, to the ten-inch-long toad, *Bufo blombergi*, of Ecuador and Colombia. The cane toad, *B. marinus*, rivals *B. blombergi* in size, but at four pounds probably wins the weight contest, so it is

Cane toad, *Bufo marinus*

considered to be the largest toad known.

True toads occur naturally around the world except for Madagascar, New Guinea, and Australia (although they have been introduced to some habitats not native to them). Most American and Asian varieties have prominent bony crests on the top of their heads. The majority, though not all, have wartlike glands on their skin. But you cannot get warts from touching toads! On each side of the head, behind the eyes, most also have a prominent gland that produces toxic chemicals to deter predators. These glands are especially prominent in the cane toad and the Colorado River toad, *B. alvarius*, which also have poison glands on their thighs. Both species produce enough toxins to dispatch any dog or cat unlucky enough to take a bite of them.

True toads are plentiful, found from temperate to tropical zones, from deserts and

African red toad, *Bufo carens*

prairies to rain forests, and from sea level to mountain tops. Most are terrestrial in habits, active at night, and reproduce in puddles, vernal ponds, or the weedy shallows of lakes and slow-moving rivers.

But there is great variety in the family. A few members spend much of their lives underground; some are totally aquatic. The climbing toads, *Pedostibes,* of Southeast Asia are tree-dwellers, while the brook toads, *Ansonia,* from the same region live along streams.

Toads typically lay very long, paired strings of eggs around vegetation in water. Those in the *Bufo* genus lay lots of tiny eggs that look a bit like poppy seeds in straw-sized gelatinous tubes. Some species can lay ten thousand to twenty thousand or more eggs. Many temperate and some tropical *Bufo* are explosive breeders, and come together in large numbers for a short breeding season. Their eggs hatch quickly into free-swimming tadpoles, and they metamorphose in two to

Golden toads, *Bufo periglenes*, with egg strings

ten weeks. Some species lay their eggs on leaves above water, and some lay eggs on land which develop directly into small toadlets, bypassing the tadpole stage.

The second largest group of toads is the harlequin frogs, genus *Atelopus,* with more than seventy-five species. They are found from Costa Rica to Bolivia, from low-elevation rain

forests to humid mountain forests up to fifteen thousand feet. They live near streams and move into the splash zones during the dry seasons.

Harlequin frogs look more like true frogs than toads. They have smooth skin, slender bodies, and long limbs, and many are brightly colored with yellow, orange or red, and black markings. High-elevation species like the Quito stubfoot toad, *Atelopus ignescens,* of the northern Andes, have dark backs and flanks. This is an adaptation for survival in the cold mountain temperatures, since basking dark-colored frogs heat up faster than light-colored frogs. *Atelopus* are active by day. They walk slowly or take small hops along the forest floor or climb into low shrubs, where they forage for a wide variety of tiny insects and spiders. Like the poison frogs, their colors tele-

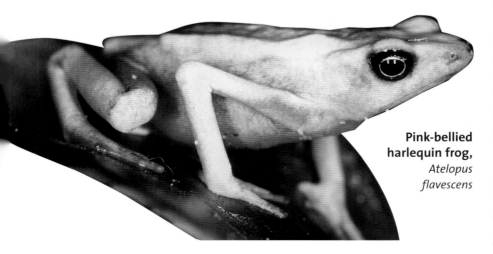

Pink-bellied harlequin frog, *Atelopus flavescens*

graph a "stay-away" warning to predators, who would do well to heed that warning. Studies of the clown frog, *A. varius,* and the harlequin frog, *A. chiriquiensis,* show that their skin produces a witch's brew of powerful toxins.

Harlequin frogs are small, one to two inches in length, but they are not timid. Both sexes are remarkably aggressive, and male-male, female-female, and female-male disputes take place often. In battle they wag their legs and arms, and chase and pounce on one another. Male-male aggression lasts longer than female-female encounters and involves chirplike calls and wrestling matches.

Males begin defending their territories well before the breeding season and will seize any passing female without the ritual of courtship. A pair may remain in amplexus for more than a month, presumably so the male can monopolize the female. As the waters of the

American green toad, *Bufo debilis*

rainy season recede, the pair travels to a stream, where the female lays strings of eggs in the water. The tadpoles have large suckerlike disc mouths, an adaptation for the stream torrents that will return in the following wet season.

These little frogs are long-lived in captivity and in nature. One group of frog biologists found a study animal more than ten years after it had originally been marked. Unfortunately, harlequin frogs have disappeared from many areas in their

range. While habitat loss may play a role, scientists have linked their disappearances to changes in weather patterns caused by global warming, which weakened their immune system. In recent times higher-elevation species have been exposed to the most extreme combinations of warm and dry conditions ever recorded. The Quito stubfoot toad and Costa Rica's golden toad, *Bufo periglenes,* have completely disappeared. Both are presumed to be extinct.

Wyoming toad, *Bufo baxteri*

Colorado River toad, *Bufo alvarius*

Family Centrolenidae
Glass Frogs

Their bodies are not really as clear as glass, but looking at the belly of a glass frog for the first time can be a startling experience. The belly skin is poorly pigmented, and you can actually see the frog's internal organs.

The topside of most glass frogs is lime green to dark green with white, yellow, blue, or red spots. They are arboreal and well camouflaged against their leafy background. Most are about one to one and one-quarter inches in length. Glass frogs are big-eyed, with the eyes directed forward, and they have expanded, somewhat T-shaped toe pads.

There are about one hundred and forty species in three genera in the family. Their habitats range from lowland moist forests to mountain rain forests from Mexico through Central America, well into South America, where the Andes are a hot spot for new species.

Fleischmann's glass frog, *Hyalinobatrachium fleischmanni,* is found from Mexico to Ecuador and Suriname. Males may be heard calling year-round in the evening

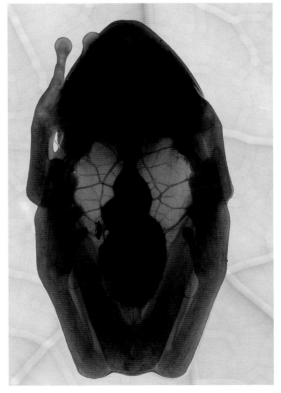

and even in the late afternoon on cloudy days. As with many of the glass frogs, the males are strongly territorial and use their calls to space themselves. Males that intrude on another male's space are warned with a short encounter call. If that doesn't work, combat starts and the newcomer is pinned down for a period of time before it is released to flee.

Breeding sites are located along a stream. When a female approaches a male's calling station, he offers encounter calls. After amplexus the female carries him on her back and moves around his territory to select an egg-laying site on the underside of a leaf overhanging the stream. She takes no more than five minutes to lay ten to fifty eggs as her partner rubs his legs over her sides and releases his sperm to fertilize the egg cluster. After resting for a couple of hours, the female leaves the breeding site and returns to the forest canopy.

The male stays close to the eggs and periodically visits them at night to keep them moist by pressing his belly and thighs against them and urinating on them. Nevertheless, many eggs dry out or are lost to parasitic frogfly and fungal attacks. After about two to four weeks the embryos that have survived hatch and drop into the water or onto the stream bank to be washed into the stream by heavy rains, where they forage in the bottom litter and muck. One high-mountain species, Buckley's giant glass frog, *Centrolene buckleyi,* lays its eggs in bromeliad plants. The territorial male stays in attendance and may guard several clutches of eggs at once.

In many glass frogs, the skin over the belly is transparent and the internal organs are visible. The slim, green, nocturnal frogs of Central and South America's humid tropical forests have large heads with big eyes and expanded "cling-on" discs on their fingers and toes.

Family Dendrobatidae
Poison Frogs

Poison frogs are living jewels. They are without question the most vividly colored amphibians in their class. But their bright, often enamel-like, colors are no mere decoration. They telegraph that the frogs are extremely toxic and to take warning.

Poison frogs produce very dangerous alkaloids in their skin. In one species, the golden poison frog, *Phyllobates terribilis*, the secretion is considered to be among the most deadly naturally occurring poisons on earth. One frog can produce enough toxin to kill ten men. These dangerous little frogs are also known as poison dart or poison arrow frogs. Their common names come from the practice of the Indians of western Colombia of coating dart and arrow tips with the frogs' skin secretions. The poison acts irreversibly on the victim's nervous system. Once wounded, there is no remedy.

The building blocks for the toxins come from the tiny insects and other minute invertebrates the frogs eat, which in turn get toxins from poisonous plants they ingest. The family includes more than two hundred species, which range in size from three quarters of an inch long to more than two inches in length. These small frogs have short but strong hind limbs and are agile climbers and jumpers. The skunk frog, appropriately named *Aromobates nocturnus*, is the giant of the poison frog

Green-and-black poison dart frog, *Dendrobates auratus*. The color pattern of each individual is distinct.

world and reaches nearly two and one-half inches in length. Unlike most of its kin, it is nocturnal, fully aquatic, and has a stinky odor.

Most poison frogs are terrestrial. They move about the forest floor and climb vegetation growing on tree trunks. They feed openly during the day, as they rarely have to concern themselves with predators. They're found in humid tropical forests from Nicaragua to Ecuador and the Amazon basin, to southeastern Brazil.

Not all so-called poison frogs are toxic. Members of the genera *Dendrobates, Phyllobates, Epipedobates,* and *Minyobates* are, but those in *Aromobates, Colostethus,* and *Mannophryne* are not. These latter frogs must be much less bold in their foraging behavior, as they are open game for many predators.

Poison frogs have a complex social, territorial, courtship, and parental care repertoire. Aggres-

sive behaviors include calling, posturing, chasing, and even wrestling. Hatching tadpoles are transported to water on the back of either the male or the female. In the strawberry poison frog, *Dendrobates pumilio,* the females lay their clutches of five to twenty eggs in moist leaf litter in the forest. Both the male and female return regularly to the nest to moisten the eggs. About a week later, hatching tadpoles are carried by the female, one to four at a time, to separate water-filled bromeliads or tree holes where they are deposited. The female returns regularly to these spots to lay an infertile egg in the water for each tadpole to eat. (She backs into the water pocket and waits for the tadpole to signal its presence by touching her vent and vibrating, thus stimulating her to release an egg.) The tadpoles transform to froglets in one and one-half to two months and become mature adults in ten months.

Left, **Granular poison frog,** *Dendrobates granuliferus*

Below, **Dyeing poison frog,** *Dendrobates tinctorius*

Poison dart frogs live in the humid regions of tropical America, from Nicaragua south to Ecuador and Brazil. They come in a kaleidoscope of colors and patterns. Their bright colors telegraph to predators that they are toxic and dangerous to eat. Most of them are terrestrial, and because they have little fear of other animals, they are active during the daytime.

Facing page:
Blue poison frog, *Dendrobates azureus*
Inset, **Yellow-banded, or bumblebee, poison frog,** *Dendrobates leucomelas*

Mimic poison frog,
Dendrobates imitator

Strawberry poison frog,
Dendrobates pumilio,
inset, right

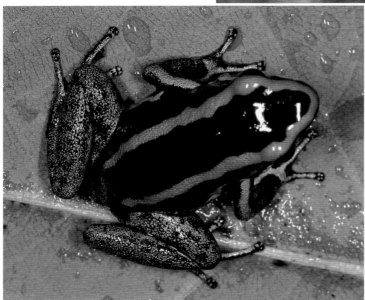

Above, **Golfodulcean poison frog,**
Phyllobates villatus

Often described as "living
jewels," the poison frogs
are the most colorful frog
family. A single species, like
the harlequin poison frogs,
Dendrobates histrionicus
(right), may display an
astonishing array of color
variations.

Family Discoglossidae
Disc-tongued Frogs

This small family, two genera with a total of eleven species, is found in Europe and northwestern Africa. They are one and one-quarter to two and three-quarters inches long, and all have disc-shaped tongues. There are five species of what are called midwife toads in the genus *Alytes,* and six painted frogs in the *Discoglossus* genus.

Midwife toads are terrestrial and look like warty-skinned toads, with slitlike vertical pupils. As might be expected from the common name, they are known for their parental care. The midwife toad, *A. obstetricans,* is representative of the group. It can be found in eight European countries, from sea level on the coast of the Iberian Peninsula to seventy-five hundred feet high in the Pyrenees Mountains.

During the breeding season, males make an explosive, high-pitched *poo, poo, poo* call every one to three seconds. The female searches out the male, which grasps her around the waist and stimulates her to lay her eggs by scratching her cloacal area with his toes. After a short time the male squeezes the female's sides, and she ejects strings of eggs. The male inseminates the eggs and then extends his legs and begins a process of wrapping the egg strings about his ankles. He may continue to breed and collect several clutches, which can

Midwife toad, *Alytes obstetricians*

total up to one hundred and fifty eggs, around his legs and waist. The male carries the eggs and keeps them moist for three to six weeks until the larvae begin to hatch. Then he transports the larvae to water, where they will continue to develop until tadpoles form. The following year the tadpoles transform into toadlets.

The Majorcan midwife toad, *A. muletensis,* is viewed as Endangered because only a small area of its mountainous habitat remains. To compound problems, the viperine snake, *Natrix maura,* was introduced to the island during Roman times and is a fierce predator of frogs and tadpoles. Another frog, *Rana perezi,* was also introduced to Majorca and is a competitor for

food. Heavy tourism and the demand for water add to a dim forecast for *A. muletensis.*

The other genus in this family, *Discoglossus,* called painted frogs, may be brightly colored and can closely resemble true frogs in appearance. Their pupils look like upside-down droplets. Female painted frogs of the species *D. pictus* lay anywhere from five hundred to a thousand eggs in an evening. The female is clasped in amplexus by a series of males during that time, and she lays small clumps of eggs until she is empty. The eggs hatch in two to ten days, and the tadpoles transform to froglets in one to three months.

Family Heleophrynidae
Ghost Frogs

Despite their eerie name, these frogs are not ghostly in appearance. The family may have gotten its common name because one of its six species is found in Skeleton Gorge, South Africa. Or perhaps the name is a result of their thin, transparent white bellies. As in the glass frogs, one can see the ghost frogs' abdominal muscles and organs through their skin.

Ghost frogs are confined to the southern tip of Africa, where they live in cool, cascading mountain streams. They are tiny creatures. The smallest forms are just over an inch long, while the biggest barely exceeds two inches. They have large eyes with vertical pupils, and their bodies are flattened. Their front feet lack webbing, but their rear feet are strongly webbed, making them good swimmers but poor jumpers. Their enlarged, triangular-shaped toe and finger pads make them well-adapted for getting into rock crevices in their stream habitat.

In reproduction the female attaches a clutch of one to two hundred eggs to a rock in the stream. As in other cold-stream tadpoles, development is slow, and metamorphosis takes about two years. Ghost frog tadpoles, like those of the tailed frogs, have a large, suckerlike mouth, which helps them graze on algae-covered rocks in the stream current. They need clean, swift-moving water to survive, and some are being threatened by habitat loss. Rose's ghost frog, *Heleophryne rosei,* is especially vulnerable because it lives in only a very small geographical area in South Africa. Global climate change—as well as the harm caused by deforestation, damming activities, and reduced stream flow—has led to habitat loss for this species. Only wise management of the now protected landscape will prevent it from becoming extinct.

Royal ghost frog, *Heleophryne regis*

Family Hemisotidae
Shovel-Nosed Frogs

The nine species in this family are well named. Other burrowing frogs use structures called tubercles on their hind feet to dig backward into the soil, but shovel-nosed frogs dig into the soil headfirst with their hard pointy snouts. They live in sub-Saharan Africa in tropical scrub forests and savannas and in well-irrigated land. These frogs have a plump, nearly cylindrical body and small eyes with vertical pupils. They are one to three inches in length, and they are picky eaters, restricting their diet to ants and termites.

The natural history of the marbled shovel-nosed frog, *Hemisus marmoratus,* is probably typical of the other members of this family. This frog comes to the surface at night before or after rainstorms or when the air is heavy with humidity. At the beginning of the rainy season,

Spotted shovel-nosed frog, *Hemisus buttatum*

the males move to the vicinity of future ponds. They may call from the surface or from their underground retreats. Their calls sound like the loud buzz produced by crickets.

A female arriving at the pond is amplexed by a male, which then secretes sticky fluids that bind them together. They remain stuck together even when the female burrows into the ground to construct an egg chamber in the bottom of the dry pond. Soon after the eggs are deposited and fertilized, the male leaves the chamber. The female rests on the eggs, and when the tadpoles hatch she remains to protect them. When rains flood the nest chambers, the tadpoles may swim to pools of water or be transported there on their mother's back to finish development.

Shovel-nosed frog, *Hemisus,* sp.

Family Hylidae
Tree Frogs

This is one of the largest frog families, with about eight hundred and fifty species spread among approximately forty genera. There is great diversity in the family, with four major groups recognized.

1. The Australia–New Guinea tree frogs. These include the water-holding frog, *Cyclorana platycephalus,* and the giant tree frog, *Litoria infrafranata.*

2. The highly arboreal leaf frogs. The familiar red-eyed tree frog, *Agalychnis callidryas,* and the waxy monkey frog, *Phyllomedusa sauvagii,* of the New World tropics belong to this second group.

3. Marsupial frogs and other related species. Marsupial frogs, like kangaroos, which carry their undeveloped young in a belly pouch, have a pouch on their backs in which eggs develop. One member of this group, *Gastrotheca guentheri,* is the only known frog with teeth on its lower jaw. Marsupial frogs in the genus *Hemiphractus* are extremely bizarre in appearance, with bony, triangular heads and long, pointed snouts. They eat other frogs and may bite when picked up.

4. American tree frogs. Some of North America's most typical and best-known frogs belong to this familiar assemblage: the green tree frog, *Hyla cinerea,* and the spring peeper, *Pseudacris crucifer.*

Tree frogs are a widespread

Barking tree frogs, *Hyla gratiosa,* in a tree hollow

family, with species appearing from North to South America, Africa, Europe, Australia, and New Guinea. They are sometimes referred to as New World tree frogs to distinguish them from another family, the Rhacophoridae, which appear mostly in Asia. But this name isn't completely accurate, as some of these New World species inconveniently turn up in Old World locations.

Generally, the hylids' habitats range from deserts to rain forests. Most species are active at night, and, of course, they are arboreal. Some live in low shrubs, others in the tree canopy, and many in between.

Some favor tree holes. The North American cricket frogs, *Acris gryllus,* are terrestrial and live near water. Species like the lowland burrowing tree frog, *Pternohyla fodiens,* of North America, and the water-holding frog of Australia are confirmed burrowers and form cocoons while underground to conserve their body moisture.

Tree frogs vary widely in size from one-half to five and one-half inches in length. They are green, yellow, or brown in color, and a number of them display flash colors on their flanks and hind limbs. Some species have the ability to change color. Their basic hues and patterns differ during the day, when they are inactive, and at night, when they are active. True to their arboreal nature, many tree frogs have long legs and enlarged adhesive finger and toe pads, which help them climb and cling to branches. They have webbed feet, and many have finger webbing as well. The frogs in the genus *Phyllomedusa* have one opposable finger, like the opposable thumb of primates and giant pandas, making it even easier for them to grasp twigs and small branches.

While most tree frogs are good climbers and strong jumpers, the leaf frogs in the family move along branches in a slow, deliberate, hand-over-hand fashion. However, some species, like the gliding leaf frog, *Agalychnis spurrelli,* can move rapidly when necessary. They take parachuting leaps with arms and legs extended and hand and toe webbing spread. They keep their flattened body and outstretched limbs parallel to the ground, which exposes the greatest amount of surface area possible and slows their fall.

Most female species in the tree frog family lay their eggs in water. In quiet waters they may attach their clutches to vegetation or spread their eggs in a thin mass on the water's surface film. Some breed in streams and attach their eggs to rocks.

Within the marsupial frogs, reproduction is specialized. Some females carry the eggs, tadpoles, or young frogs exposed on their back or hidden in a pouch on their back. After brooding, some of the pouched frogs take their tadpoles to water, where their

The tree frog family, Hylidae, has more than 800 members. Most are slender with long legs, webbed feet, and enlarged adhesive discs on their fingers and toes for climbing on plants at night. Marsupial frog, *Gastrotheca marsupiata*, below; casque-headed tree frog, *Triprion spatulatus*, right.

Perhaps the most handsome North American hylid, the ornate chorus frog, *Pseudacris ornata,* above, lacks large toe discs and does little climbing in its southern cypress and pine barrens pond habitats. By contrast, the Cuban tree frog, *Osteopilus septentrionalis,* right and below, has exceptionally large toe discs and is a superb climber.

development is lengthy. It may be two to four months before tadpoles transform into froglets.

Male gladiator tree frogs, *Hyla boans,* are another well-named species. They range in the Amazon and Orinoco river basins. At breeding time the male finds the soft earth near streams and constructs depressions, which then fill with water. At night the males come to these depressions to call females. The breeding male will aggressively challenge other males with rapid charges and chases. Sometimes these encounters end in violent wrestling matches, and the combatants stab at each other with an unsheathed spine they carry on each thumb. Eyes and eardrums are targets, and many males are wounded from battles during the breeding season. The females are more sensible and are never involved in these skirmishes.

Our most familiar tree frog, the spring peeper, *Pseudacris crucifer,* below, is the harbinger of spring across its North American range. Its deafening, sleigh-bell-like chorus often begins before the ice leaves the breeding ponds. Above, an unusually netlike patterned clown tree frog, *Hyla leucophyllata,* from the Upper Amazon basin. Inset, right, pine woods tree frog, *Hyla femoralis,* of the southeastern United States; and tropical American red-eyed tree frogs, *Agalychnis callidryas,* opposite.

Commonly known as African tree frogs, members of the reed and sedge frog family look similar to tropical American tree frogs, with their long, slender legs and enlarged discs on the toes, equipment for arboreal life. Above, reed frog, *Hyperolius,* in flight. Spotted reed frog, *Hyperolius puncticulatus,* of East Africa, inset, right.

Red-legged running frog, *Kassina maculata*

Family Hyperoliidae
Reed and Sedge Frogs

This family of small to medium-sized, brightly colored frogs has more than two hundred and fifty species in nineteen genera, most of them found south of the Sahara in Africa. There are an additional dozen species, the Madagascar reed frogs, in the genus *Heterixalus,* and a single species in the Seychelles Islands, *Tachycnemis seychellensis.*

These frogs are smooth skinned, many of them so smooth they look enameled. They are found in the reeds and rushes surrounding lakes, swamps, and ponds, even within urban areas. Most are arboreal, but some live on the ground, like the Senegal running frog, *Kassina senegalensis.* This nocturnal species and its relatives do not hop or jump like many frogs do. Instead, they walk or run through savannas and open grasslands on short, thin hind legs. Their striped bodies blend in well with the surrounding grasses. When the dry season comes, they sleep through the warm weather in burrows in the mud.

Though it is basically nocturnal like the others in this family, the spotted reed frog, *Hyperolius puncticulatus,* of East Africa will often sit on a stream bank and sunbathe for hours. There are more than one hundred and twenty species of *Hyperolius* found throughout the continent. They sleep during the dry months and emerge only when the rains begin, to devour mosquitoes and gnats. Many of the sedge frogs lay eggs in foam or bubble nests, but most species lay their eggs in water or on submerged aquatic plants.

Other members of this family have a variety of egg-laying habits. In the leaf-folding frogs, *Afrixalus,* mating pairs fold leaves together with their legs and glue them with secretions from the female to hold the eggs. When the tadpoles hatch, they fall into the water below the nest. The African wart frog, *Acanthixalus spinosus,* lays its eggs in holes in trees. Forest tree frogs and bush frogs lay their eggs in depressions in the ground near water. The tadpoles hatch during heavy rains and wriggle their way to water.

Golden leaf-folding frog,
Afrixalus aureus

Family Leiopelmatidae
New Zealand Frogs

New Zealand's native frogs are considered to be truly ancient creatures. These small amphibians are similar to frogs that lived in the shadow of dinosaurs during the Jurassic period and appear to have remained unchanged for about 200 million years. They are one and one-quarter to two inches in length, brown or green in color, lack an external eardrum and a vocal pouch, and have smooth skin on the bottoms of their feet. Because they share skeletal and tail-wagging muscle characteristics with the tailed frogs of the Pacific Northwest, some authorities believe they are closely related. More likely, the two families represent two primitive lines of frogs that inherited their features from distant ancestors.

Fossil remains indicate that frogs were once widely found in New Zealand on both North and South islands, but today they are among the rarest of frogs. The largest species *Leiopelma waitomoensis,* which reached four inches, has vanished, as have all the frogs that once inhabited South Island.

On New Zealand's North Island, Hochstetter's frog, *L. hochstetteri,* is the most common of the survivors. It is found in several areas on the north end, along cool, clear, shaded streams at altitudes up to 2600 feet and clearly has the most aquatic habits of the group. As with the other New Zealand frogs, it is nocturnal. During the day it hides in wet cavities or under stones and logs. Archey's frog, *L. archeyi,* is known only from the

Hochstetter's frog, *Leiopelma hochstetteri*

Coromandel Peninsula of North Island, where it is found at similar elevations with Hochstetter's frog but prefers open forest or misty ridges. The Stephen's Island, or Hamilton's frog, *L. hamiltoni,* and the Maud Island frog, *L. pakeka,* are found on their respective tiny islands, both in Cook Strait between North and South islands. There are no other native frogs living in New Zealand.

During the breeding season male New Zealand frogs often arrive at the egg-laying sites weeks before eggs are laid. They do not chorus, and they do not have an advertisement call, but they do make an open-mouth squeak or chirp when they are distressed or in the midst of breeding. The male amplexes the female in a fashion similar to that of the tailed frog. He holds her with his arms tightly wrapped about her waist just in front of her rear legs. This process, known as inguinal

Beyond Vocalization

Vocalizations are frogs' most important means of communication, and distinct types of calls are used in different behavioral contexts. But vocalizations are not the only way frogs communicate. Researchers have found that the ancient, voiceless Hamilton's frog, *L. hamiltoni,* communicates chemically through feces. These frogs prefer the odor of their own feces and the odors of familiar frogs that share their home range, but try to avoid the odors of unfamiliar kin. What information is signaled through the feces—size, fitness, sex? The studies are ongoing. But this discovery of chemical communication in frogs offers a window on how primitive frogs may have signaled one another before vocalizations evolved. It may also mean that another level of frog communication is generally taking place that remains to be deciphered.

amplexus, is considered to be a primitive breeding trait. Females lay small clutches of large unpigmented eggs in strings on land and in damp locations, under rotting logs or stones, or in shallow pockets of water. The males attend the eggs while they are developing.

New Zealand frogs undergo direct development, bypassing the tadpole stage. However, the tiny froglets hatch before they have completed development. Hochstetter's froglets move to a stream to complete their metamorphosis. The tiny froglets of the other New Zealand species climb onto the backs of their parents and complete their development there. It may take them an additional three to four years to reach adulthood.

The arrival of humans, and the rats and other exotic predators they brought with them, has been fatal to several of the New Zealand frogs. Those that remain are threatened by habitat destruction, including logging on North Island, predators, and

Hamilton's frog, *Leiopelma hamiltoni*

the consequences of being in small, isolated populations. The Stephen's Island frog is thought to be one of the world's most endangered species. The population is believed to be fewer than one hundred and fifty frogs living in a one-fifteenth-acre rock pile, colloquially known as the "frog bank." To help ensure the survival of the Stephen's Island frog, it has been introduced successfully to Motuara Island, a rat-free site in the Cook

Strait. The Maud Island frog is much more secure, with a population estimated as high as nineteen thousand.

Recent sophisticated genetic studies found that the Maud Island and Stephen's Island frogs are really the same species. Nevertheless, they do have differences because of the length of time they have been geographically separated, and both populations need to be managed carefully.

Southern bell frog, *Litoria raniformis*

Whistling tree frog, *Litoria ewingi*

Family Leptodactylidae
Southern Frogs

South American bullfrog,
Leptodactylus pentadactylus

This is the largest of all the frog families and one that displays some interesting behaviors. The Colombian horned frog, *Ceratophrys calcarata,* for example, has been seen wiggling its toes behind its head to lure prey. There are about 1130 species in fifty genera in the family, and that number grows steadily.

The leptodactylids, as they are often called, are found from Arizona and Texas to Chile and Argentina, as well as in the West Indies. They range from one-half inch to a grand nine inches in size and can be found from sea level to above timberline, where they lead aquatic, terrestrial, arboreal, or burrowing lives, depending on the species. Some are toadlike, others look like typical frogs, and some have big toe discs like tree frogs.

Because of the great diversity in the family, it is difficult to give the family a common name that fits well. The largest number of them, some seven hundred species, belong to the "rain frogs," genus *Eleutherodactylus.* Representatives include the greenhouse frog, *E. planirostris,* and the Puerto Rican coqui, *E. coqui,* both of which have been introduced into Florida and Louisiana from Cuba and Puerto Rico, respectively.

Nearly all rain frogs lay their eggs on land, and the eggs undergo direct development into tiny froglets, while attended by a parent. The Puerto Rican frog, *E. jasperi,* is an exception; it has internal fertilization and bears its young alive.

Perhaps the most bizarrely shaped leptodactylid is the Lake Titicaca frog, *Telmatobius culeus,* which inhabits lakes at thirteen thousand feet in the Andes of Bolivia and Peru. It is fully aquatic and lays its eggs in lake shallows. The frog's flattened body looks as though it is covered with a baggy skin several sizes too large for it. Oxygen is rare in the lakes where it lives, so it needs the extra skin, with its many folds and blood vessels, to "breathe" efficiently.

The best known leptodactylids are probably those that are popular as pets—the horned frogs, the Brazilian, *Ceratophrys cornuta,* and the ornate, *C. ornata,* among them. For dinner these big, nocturnal, pot-bellied frogs sit and wait, half-buried in the forest litter, and ambush passing prey. Other frogs, lizards, snakes, and rodents are considered tasty morsels, as well as large invertebrates.

Ornate horned frog,
Ceratophrys ornata

Lake Titicaca frog, *Telmatobius culeus*, in amplexus

The smokey jungle frog, or South American bullfrog, *Leptodactylus pentadactylus,* and the mountain chicken frog, *L. fallax,* are big fellows and also take lots of vertebrates, including small birds and bats. They themselves are considered fine dining by humans. Yes, they do taste like chicken!

The *Leptodactylus* are primarily terrestrial. To make their foam nests, they use their rear legs to whip up the egg gelatin and mucus they secrete from their bodies. The huge nest they create is usually set in a dry depression near a pool that will be flooded by rain. The female lays her clutch of a thousand eggs in the nest, which serves to protect the eggs from drying out until they hatch. Tadpoles are washed from the nest into a nearby flooded body of water.

Initially the tadpoles eat the foam in the nest, but when they become free swimming they eat frog eggs, other tadpoles, and plant material.

Smokey jungle frogs have a variety of defenses against predators. If they are approached by a predator, they inflate and lift themselves with their arms and legs, presenting their toxin-producing back and groin. When grabbed, they produce large amounts of mucus, which makes them hard to hold. If you pick one of these frogs up, toxins that waft from the mucus may cause irritation of your own mucous membranes, causing swollen eyes and heavy sneezing. Direct contact often causes a rash. If all defense fails and the frog is attacked, it usually emits a very loud, high-pitched scream.

Greenhouse frog,
Eleutherodactylus planirostris

Family Mantellidae
Mantellid Frogs

This interesting family exists only on the large island of Madagascar off the east coast of Africa. There are more than one hundred and fifty species in three major genera: *Mantella, Mantidactylus,* and the bright-eyed frogs, *Boophis,* which closely resemble tree frogs. Most are terrestrial, but there are aquatic and burrowing varieties.

The mantellids range in size from less than an inch to about four inches in length. Reproductive strategies vary from the typical scenario as seen in *Boophis*—laying eggs directly in water from which tadpoles develop—to the behavior of *Mantella,* whose members lay clutches of about one hundred eggs in damp pockets in the surface litter. Tadpoles then wash into streams during high waters. There are also examples of direct development, in which the tadpole stage is skipped. *Mantidactylus* deposit their egg clusters on leaves overhanging water, and hatching tadpoles drop into the pools below to continue their development.

Unlike most frogs, *Mantidactylus* do not engage in amplexus during mating. Instead, the male places his thighs over the head of the female, and she immediately begins to shed eggs without help from her partner. His sperm are released onto her back

Green-and-black mantella,
Mantella nigricans

and flow over the eggs. The most remarkable members of this family are the Malagasy poison frogs, of the *Mantella* genus. They are the living jewels of the Old World and represent a dramatic case of convergent evolution with the poison frogs of South America, the dendro- batids. Like them, the Malagasy frogs are vividly colored and have the same small stature and shape. And they also produce toxic skin secretions.

Mantellas are often found in remnant forests that are quickly

Ornate mantella,
Mantella expectata

Golden mantella, *Mantella aurantiaca*

being lost to deforestation and dramatic alteration of landscapes. As a result, many populations of Malagasy poison frogs are crashing. To compound problems, mantellas have also become very popular in the pet trade, and many thousands have been removed from their dwindling habitats to meet that demand. The ornate *M. expectata,* the golden *M. aurantiaca,* the harlequin *M. cowanii,* and Bernhard's *M. bernhardi* are Critically Endangered. It is not likely that these and other highly attractive species with small distributions will long survive man's relentless drive to capture and own them.

Painted mantella,
Mantella madagascariensis

Malayan horned frog,
Megophrys nasuta

Family Megophryidae
Asian Toadfrogs

This medium-sized family of about one hundred and thirty frogs is another ancient group. It is found in India, throughout Southeast Asia, and on many islands, including Borneo, Sumatra, Java, and the Philippines. They are the largest and most ecologically diverse frogs in the region. Toadfrogs range from about one to five inches in length and display a wide variety of body shapes. They merge well with their environment, their colors and shapes mimicking the dead leaves of their forest floor habitat. For example, the horned frog of Malaysia, *Megophrys nasuta*, is brilliantly camouflaged with horny pro-jections above its eyes, mottled brown coloration, and skin projections that look like the veins on leaves.

Asian toadfrogs are poor jumpers and prefer to walk about their terrestrial habitat. Large horned frogs put up a good front when faced with predators. They inflate their lungs, elevate their bodies, open their mouths and scream, and jump at the adversary.

During the breeding season *Megophrys* sit in water and conspicuously announce their presence with a loud clank call. They lay their eggs in quiet waters, and their tadpoles, equipped with a funnel-shaped mouth on top of the head, feed on the surface of water. Some toadfrogs breed in swift-moving streams. They have tadpoles with very muscular tails, reduced fins, and a large suckerlike mouth—all adaptations for life in the fast lane.

Siamese leaf frog, *Megophrys longipes*

Family Microhylidae
Narrow-Mouthed Frogs

There are more than three hundred and sixty species of these teardrop-shaped frogs in more than sixty genera. Geographically, they are a very diverse group, ranging in the United States, throughout South America, in Africa, India, Southeast Asia, New Guinea, and northern Australia. They can be found in many different habitats, from dry deserts to the wettest rain forests, and they may be terrestrial, arboreal, or subterranean.

Most varieties are small, varying from less than an inch in length to three and one-half inches—with round bodies and narrow mouths. Nevertheless, there are differences in body plan, according to the species' lifestyle. Burrowers have flattened bodies and pointed

Tomato frog, *Dyscophus antongilii*

snouts, and arboreal species have large toe discs. The fat-looking African frogs in the genus *Breviceps* are so plump and have such short limbs that the males cannot hold on to the females during breeding, so they use a body glue, which is produced in glands onto their belly, to stick themselves onto the females. One of the most distinctive in appearance is

Madagascar's tomato frog, *Dyscophus antongilii.* No dull green color here; it is bright red.

The Great Plains narrow-mouthed toad, *Gastrophryne olivacea* (whose common name is "toad," but it is really a frog), has a very unusual relationship with the Texas tarantula. They live together! They share a large spider hole and hunt in the same area. The tarantula recognizes the toad through chemical cues and does not attack its housemate. However, other frogs in the neighborhood must beware, as the tarantula will quickly include them in its diet.

Eastern narrowmouth toad,
Gastrophryne carolinensis

Asiatic painted frog,
Kaloula pulchra

Family Myobatrachidae
Australian Frogs

Australia, New Guinea, and Tasmania are home to this assemblage of frogs, with more than one hundred and twenty species in twenty-three genera. Most are found in Australia, where they are the country's dominant terrestrial frogs. They range in size from three quarters of an inch to about four inches. Some are dry grassland species, others are found in the rain forest, and still others live in marshes or along cool mountain streams, as well as in most habitats in between. There are no tree dwellers, however.

Since so much of Australia is arid, it is not surprising that many of these frogs are burrowers, like the crucifix frog, *Notaden bennettii,* and the trilling frog, *Neobatrachus centralis.* Both species are short-legged and squat, with a digging spade on each ankle. The turtle

Crucifix frog, *Notaden bennettii*

frog, *Myobatrachus gouldi,* is molelike in appearance, with a small head and eyes and over-sized hands and fingers. It leads a subterranean life and digs deep tunnels headfirst. Its eggs are deposited in moist sand as deep as three feet below the surface, where they undergo direct development.

At the opposite end of the scale is the Australian bullfrog, *Limnodynastes dumerili,* which lays upward of four thousand eggs in a floating foam nest. Depending on the local condi-

tions, development may take four to fifteen months. The female pouched, or hip-pocket frog, *Assa darlingtoni,* lays a small clutch of eggs on the ground, and the male allows hatching tadpoles to climb onto his back and into hip pouches, where they develop for about two months before exiting as miniatures of the adults.

In 1973 a frog that has extremely unusual reproductive habits was first described: This is the gastric-brooding frog, *Rheobatrachus silus.* Eleven years later a second gastric-brooding species was discovered, *R. vitellinus.* The females of these species turn off the digestive juices in their stomachs and swallow the fertilized eggs. The tadpoles develop in the female's stomach, and after six or seven weeks, up to twenty-five young are born. In a twist of fate, both gastric-brooding frogs went extinct in the 1980s before biologists could get to fully know them.

Turtle frog, *Myobatrachus gouldi*

Family Pelobatidae
Spadefoot Toads

The spadefoots are well named because they are digging champions. They have a sharp-edged, horny black spade on each hind foot which they use to rapidly burrow vertically downward into the soil. With their short-legged, squatty appearance, they resemble true toads in general body form. But spadefoots have large eyes with vertical cat-eye pupils and smooth skin, in contrast to true toads, which are warty and have round pupils.

Plains spadefoot, *Spea bombifrons*

There are eleven species in three genera in the family, all one to two and one-half inches long. The genera *Spea* and *Scaphiopus* occur in North America, and *Pelobates* in Eurasia. Spadefoots are nocturnal and spend almost all of their days underground. Most prefer dry habitats with sandy soils, and they have developed strategies that permit them to survive the longest droughts. On warm humid nights during the summer they emerge from their burrows to feed but do not travel very far, preferring to sit and wait for prey to come to them.

The North American spadefoots are explosive breeders. Perhaps stimulated by the noise of falling rain or its vibrations on the hard soil, they have a burst of energy during summer thunderstorms. Breeding choruses may be deafening, and the spadefoots sometimes combine their voices with those of toads sharing the same pool. Their eggs are laid in temporary pools, and clutch size may exceed three thousand eggs. Some species have an extraordinarily short development time: Couch's spadefoot, *Scaphiopus couchii*, develops from egg to frog in eight days! On the other hand, the common European spadefoot, *Paelobates fuscus,* requires a significantly longer development time; their tadpoles may overwinter. Depending upon environmental conditions, the tadpoles of the Plains spadefoot, *Spea bombifrons,* may assume two different forms—a large fast-growing carnivorous type or a smaller slow-growing tadpole.

Couch's spadefoot, *Scaphiopus couchii*

Parsley frog, *Pelodytes punctatus*

Family Pelodytidae
Parsley Frogs

The parsley frog, *Pelodytes punctatus,* is well camouflaged. It is also very well named; its backside looks like it is garnished with a few sprigs of parsley. There are only three species in the family, and all of them share the same genus. Unfortunately, there are far more fossil parsley frogs than there are living varieties. Fossil remains have been reported from scattered locations in Europe and North America, while living parsley frogs are found only in Western Europe and the Caucasus Mountains.

Parsley frogs are small (about one and one-half inches), big-eyed, and warty-skinned. They share a number of characteristics with members of the spadefoot family but lack their digging spade and have different skeletal features. The Caucasian parsley frog, *P. caucasicus,* prefers cool, shaded habitats along the shores of clear ponds and streams in mountain forests, while the Iberian parsley frog, *P. ibericus,* is more flexible in its habitat requirements. It lives anywhere from open areas near the sea to about three thousand feet in the mountains. Parsley frogs lead a subterranean existence and forage on the surface after dark. However, during the breeding season they are also active during the day. This breeding season is a very long affair, months in length, and triggered by rainfall.

At breeding time males arrive at the breeding pools and begin calling. Females produce one hundred to one thousand eggs, which they lay in small portions. The tadpoles may undergo transformation in two to three months, or they may overwinter and complete metamorphosis the following year. The froglets mature in two to three years.

The health of two of the three parsley frog species is not clear, but *P. punctatus* is considered to be Endangered or Vulnerable in all the countries in which it resides. Drainage of marshlands, canalization of rivers, and habitat fragmentation are believed to be the causes of the population decline.

Family Pipidae
Tongueless Frogs

This is an unusual family of thirty sub-Saharan and tropical South American species, all of which lack a tongue. They have a bony voice box with two rods that produce a clicking sound, which signals their presence to their neighbors. They also have a lateral line system like the one in fish, which detects vibrations in the water. Most species live in ponds, streams, roadside ditches, or any of a wide variety of quiet aquatic habitats, where they grab small fish, tadpoles, and invertebrates and stuff them into their mouth.

All Pipidae are designed for a highly aquatic existence. Their bodies are flattened, and their legs extend laterally from their body, so movement on land is difficult. Their legs are long, and their feet are fully webbed. In the African clawed frog, *Xenopus laevis,* the fingers end in clawlike tips, while the fingertips of the

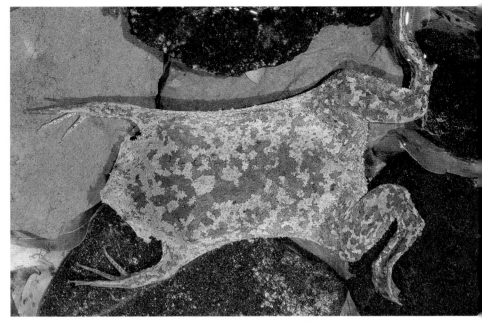

Surinam toad, *Pipa pipa*

Surinam toad, *Pipa pipa,* and other members of the *Pipa* genus end in a star-shaped sensory structure. The pipid frogs have small eyes that sit on top of the head and point upward, the better to peer out of their watery habitats.

The African clawed frogs are amazingly adaptive, flourishing in habitats ranging from mountain streams to sewage treatment plants. Because of this flexibility, *Xenopus laevis* can quickly become a pest when introduced into places it doesn't belong. In the 1930s they began to be exported around the world for use in pregnancy tests, later were used as a laboratory standard, and ultimately as a pet. Large numbers have appeared in the American Southwest, and they have been banned from California, Arizona, and some other states. They breed over a period of several months and lay their eggs singly on stones and aquatic vegetation. The eggs hatch in three or four days, and the tadpoles, which have long barbels that give them the appearance of catfish, suspend themselves in water, where they feed on microscopic life.

African clawed frog, *Xenopus laevis*

Pseudidae
Paradox Frogs

Imagine a ten-inch tadpole transforming into a two-and-one-half-inch frog. A paradox? Indeed. The paradox frog, *Pseudis paradoxa*, holds the record for the largest tadpole, but at the end of metamorphosis it is a very ordinary-sized frog.

There are nine species in the paradox frog family, found in the lowlands of northern and eastern South America, from Colombia to Argentina. They are well designed for an aquatic existence, with eyes perched on top of the head. They have strong legs and long, slender, fully webbed toes for swimming. Their long digits stir up

Paradox frog, *Pseudis paradoxa*

the silt and debris on the bottom of ponds and ditches as they forage for prey. The paradox frog is active night and day and can be seen floating amid aquatic vegetation. Breeding seems to be related to sudden rainfall, and their greenish eggs are laid in frothy masses between plants along the shoreline. The tadpoles spend four months reaching their enormous size before turning into regular-sized frogs.

Pseudis minuta

Family Ranidae
True Frogs

As the common name of this family suggests, its members have the general appearance you would expect to see in a frog: a slender, streamlined body; smooth, moist skin; long webbed hind legs; a large tympanum behind the eye; and a slim waist. There are more than seven hundred and thirty species of true frogs, and they occur almost around the world. (They are absent from the West Indies and most oceanic islands, and have limited numbers in South America and Australia.)

True frogs range in size from the biggest—the West African goliath frog, *Conraua goliath,* at twelve inches—to the micro frog, *Microbatrachella capensis,* of southern Africa, which measures less than an inch in length. They are primarily brown or green with darker markings, and they

American bullfrog, *Rana catesbeiana*

have the widest range of habitats of all the frog families, from dry areas to rain forests to temperate regions at high altitudes.

Some of North America's best-known frogs fall into this family, and all twenty-seven representatives found north of Mexico are in one genus, *Rana.* Its members include the Ameri-

can bullfrog, *R. catesbeiana;* the northern leopard frog, *R. pipiens;* the pig frog, *R. grylio;* and the wood frog, *R. sylvatica.*

Adult true frogs are primarily aquatic, living in and around permanent ponds and pools. During the breeding season the males of many ranids develop rough, swollen pads on their thumbs to help them hold on to females during amplexus. Most lay their eggs in water, and the tadpoles metamorphose into juvenile frogs.

There are many exceptions to the general rules of lifestyle and reproduction in this broad family, however. Some populations of the European edible frog, *R. esculenta,* exhibit a modified form of cyclical parthenogenesis, which means they alternate between sexual and asexual reproduction. The North Amer-

Northern leopard frog, *Rana pipiens*

ican wood frog, *R. sylvatica,* and its European counterpart, the common frog, *R. temporaria,* breed as soon as the ice is gone from their breeding pools. They lay their eggs in communal clusters. If it is a large colony, the collection may be huge. Chirping frogs in the African genus *Arthroleptella* lay small clutches of eggs in a ground nest cavity.

The Fiji tree frog, *Platymantis vitiensis,* has expanded toe pads for climbing trees and jumping from limb to limb, while those of its terrestrial relative, the Fiji ground frog, *P. vitiana,* are modest in size. African sand frogs, *Tomopterna,* look more like toads than true frogs—complete with spades on their hind feet—and they are burrowers. Torrent or cascade frogs, *Amolops,* range throughout Southeast Asia and are adapted to life in fast-flowing rain forest streams. The tadpole stage has a suckerlike disc on its

African bullfrog,
Pyxicephalus adspersus

bottom, which helps it cling to rocks in swift water.

This family is really a confusing taxonomic jumble with many inconsistencies, and genera will likely come and go as the science of grouping things improves.

Some true frogs are facing serious conservation dilemmas.

The Tablas Island wrinkled frog, *Platymantes levigatus,* and the Negros cave frog, *P. spelaeus,* are Critically Endangered in the altered landscapes of their Philippine habitats. In our own backyard the Tarahumara frog, *R. tarahumarae,* has vanished from Arizona, where the last individual was seen in 1983, although it continues to survive in northwestern Mexico. The Ramsey Canyon leopard frog, *R. subaquavocalis,* known for its underwater calls, is found only in the Huachuca Peak area of Arizona. Perhaps one hundred breeding adults survive.

Striped phase of the North American wood frog, *Rana sylvatica,* from the northwestern part of its range

"True frogs" are the most familiar of the North American frogs. Their voices are often heard around ponds and lakes on warm evenings. The ranids have the largest distribution of all frog families and live around the globe. The pig frog, *Rana grylio*, upper left; green frog, *R. clamitans*, above; and gopher frog, *R. capito*, left, are North American representatives.

Solomon Island eyelash frog, *Ceratobatrachus guentheri*, bottom left; Natal chirping frog, *Arthroleptella hewitti*, bottom right.

Eared tree frog,
Rhacophorus rufipes

Family Rhacophoridae
Old World Tree Frogs

Although they are believed to be most closely related to the true frogs of the Ranidae family, the Old World tree frogs also have similarities to the New World frogs of the Hylidae family. Like them, they are arboreal and have enlarged toe pads at the ends of their fingers to aid in climbing. In general, however, these tree frogs are larger than the hylids and have flattened bodies.

There are about two hundred and twenty species, which range from a tiny three quarters of an inch in length, to four and three-quarter inches. The majority are native to tropical areas of Asia and are seen from India and Sri Lanka to Japan. Most of the Asian species have large eyes with horizontal pupils, and they appear in colors from green to brown and gray to black and white. Many have bright flash colors on the inner thighs, which they expose as they leap away from potential predators. The patterns of gaudy colors are meant to confuse predators by distorting the frog's body pattern. The flying frogs, genus *Rhacophorus,* have extensive webbing between their toes, which they extend as they leap and parachute to another perch in the rain forest canopy.

While some species lay their eggs directly in water, many of the Asian tree frogs lay their eggs in foam nests, in water or in trees above pools, from which newly hatched tadpoles drop into the water to continue their development. Some bubble-nest frogs in the genus *Philautus* lay small clutches of eggs in trees.

There are no tadpoles; tiny froglets emerge from the eggs.

In the African foam-nest species several males will gather around a female in branches above water during the breeding season and with their hind legs whip up the fluid that accompanies the eggs, contributing some of their own body secretions. The resulting large foam nest hardens and protects the eggs until they hatch and the tadpoles drop into the water. Other species lay eggs in tree holes, where tadpoles develop.

At least one of the Old World tree frogs is currently Endangered, Schumaker's bubble-nest frog, *Philautus schmackeri,* which is from Mindoro Island in the Philippines. Severe changes in its habitat are to blame.

Some members of the Old World tree frog family have webbing that extends to the tips of their fingers and toes. The webbing acts as a parachute and slows their drop as the frogs "fly" or "glide" to a lower perch. Left, Java flying frog, *Rhacophorus reinwardtii;* middle, Perak bubble-nest frog, *Philautus vermiculatus;* below, Chinese gliding frog, *Polypedates dennysii.*

Family Rhinodermatidae
Mouth-Brooding Frogs

There is just one genus and two species of small "rhinoceros snouted" frogs in this unusual family: One species is called Darwin's frog, *Rhinoderma darwinii,* and the other is known only by its scientific name, *R. rufum.* They inhabit temperate forests of southern Chile and Argentina and are placed in their own family largely because of their mouth-brooding behavior. These terrestrial frogs deposit small numbers of eggs on moist ground. One or more males may remain in attendance around a clutch while the eggs quickly develop. After two or three weeks the tadpoles hatch and are picked up in the mouths of waiting males. The male may carry five to fifteen of the tiny larvae. In *R. rufum,* the tadpoles are taken directly to pools of water, where they are released. Male *R. darwinii* keep the tadpoles in their vocal sac for about fifty days, during which time they transform to froglets and are then released.

Darwin's frog, *Rhinoderma darwinii*

Family Rhinophrynidae
Burrowing Toad

The Mexican burrowing toad, *Rhinophrynus dorsalis,* is one of a kind and in its own family. Fossil evidence shows that about 37 million years ago, related species lived as far north as Canada. This plump, almost shapeless, loose-skinned frog has a small head with tiny eyes and a well-developed spade on each hind ankle for digging backward into the soil. It is about three inches long and dark brown or black with a reddish orange stripe down the middle of the back.

The burrowing toad fancies ants and termites when feeding. Unlike most frogs, which open their mouths and flip their tongues onto prey, this toad catches small insects by sticking its tongue out through a small opening at the front of the mouth.

Heavy rain stimulates breeding behavior and brings the toads out of their subterranean hideouts. The males gather around temporary pools, where they float on the surface in large breeding choruses. Their call is unique. The Mayan name for the frog is *ou* because of the loud, long, ascending *uooooooooo* sound it makes. After amplexus by the male, the female will lay several thousand eggs, which hatch into tadpoles in a few days.

Family Scaphiophrynidae
Madagascar Narrow-Mouthed Frogs

The nine members of this family are found only in Madagascar, and all but one species belong to the genus *Scaphiophryne*. (They are often grouped in a subfamily with other narrow-mouthed frogs in the Family Microhylidae. Scaphiophrynid tadpoles share characteristics with both the true frog and narrow-mouthed frog families.) Madagascar narrow-mouthed frogs are one to two inches long and found in savannas, mountains, and rain forests, where they breed and lay large numbers of tiny eggs in quiet temporary pools. The striking red, light green, and black Gottlebe's narrow-mouthed frog, *S. gottlebei,* the most colorful member of the family has become popular in the pet trade. Thousands are captured each year for this purpose. Their fingers have large toe pads, and there is a horny tubercle on the underside of each hind foot. These features help them dig quickly into the substrate or climb the walls of the canyons where they live.

Gottlebe's narrow-mouthed frog,
Scaphiophryne gottlebei

Family Sooglossidae
Seychelles Frogs

This small family survived the geological breakup of India and the Seychelles Islands 65 million years ago. The four secretive species live only on Mahe and Silhouette, around granite boulders at high elevations in rain forests with deep leaf litter. Seychelles frogs appear to be most closely related to the newly discovered purple burrowing frog described earlier. They measure about one-half to one and one-half inches long, and males are smaller than females. Gardiner's Seychelles frog, *Sooglossus gardineri,* is the most common and widespread, and at half an inch one of the world's smallest frogs. Thomasset's frog, *Neosmantis thomasseti,* the largest and rarest of the four, lives in the highest moist forests.

Seychelles frogs all look quite similar but can be identified by their advertisement calls. *S. gardineri* males sing one finely toned note lasting a fraction of a second, somewhat like the chirp of a cricket. *S. pipilodryas* has a similar call, but its high-pitched squeak is repeated six times. Male *S. sechellensis* and *N. thomasseti* sing complex calls—rare among frogs—a primary note followed by about four short secondary notes and then a four second call. The function of their calls is not known. They increase during the breeding season and following wet weather, so they presumably attract mates.

Females lay their eggs in a terrestrial nest. It is believed that the female guards them. *S. sechellensis* eggs hatch after two to three weeks. Then the tad-

Gardiner's Seychelles frog,
Sooglossus gardineri

poles climb onto the female's back and remain there during metamorphosis. The eggs of *S. gardineri* take about another week to develop and hatch directly into froglets. *S. gardineri* eats tiny mites, fly larvae, ants, and small crustaceans. This species probably does not compete with its larger relatives, which can eat bigger items. Given their restricted habitats and range, Seychelles frogs face an uncertain future. Thomasset's frog is Endangered, and the others are Vulnerable.

CHAPTER SIX

A FADING CHORUS

IT READS LIKE A MYSTERY NOVEL, but so far it's a story without an ending. Something is killing frogs and other amphibians the world over. At the First World Congress of Herpetology, held in 1989 in Canterbury, England, scientists became alarmed by the widespread number of reports of amphibian populations that were declining, or had disappeared altogether, and of amphibians with deformities. Frogs and other amphibians are very sensitive to changes in their surroundings, especially to the quality of the air and the water in their environments. If the ponds and streams in which they live as tadpoles and to which the adults return to breed are filled with silt from housing developments or laden with toxic chemicals from manufacturing plants, the health of the frogs and toads will be affected as will the health of humans.

In the United States—which is home to some ninety frog and toad species, and one hundred and forty species of salamanders—amphibian abnormalities and deformities, such as extra or missing limbs or eyes, have been documented in forty-four states. Serious declines in frog populations have been reported in California, the Rocky Mountains, the Southwest, and Puerto Rico. And we are not alone. Australia and Central America are also experiencing severe amphibian declines.

Extinction is a natural process. Species have been appearing and disappearing for eons. Natural fluctuations in the numbers of frog populations can account for some of the disappearances, particularly in species that have small ranges or are dependent on specialized environments, but they cannot be the explanation for the widespread declines of many populations around the world. Today, most extinctions are caused by the activities of humans.

Chemically Caused Gender Confusion

Farmers in the Corn Belt of the midwestern United States use a chemical herbicide called atrazine to kill weeds that invade fields planted with the nation's leading export crops: corn and soybeans. Atrazine has been used on crops since 1956. More than 60 million pounds of the herbicide were applied during 2001. In 2002 Dr. Tyrone B. Hayes, associate professor of integrative biology at the University of California, Berkeley, and his colleagues discovered that when exposed to atrazine at minute levels, tadpoles of the northern leopard frog, *Rana pipiens*, become hermaphrodites—creatures with both male and female sex organs. The herbicide also lowers levels of the male hormone testosterone in sexually mature male frogs to amounts lower than those found in normal female frogs. The affected male leopard frogs are unable to reproduce. The same chemical has been found in tap water in the Midwest.

Unfortunately, it does not seem that scientists will find one thing to explain all the frog deaths, deformities, and disappearances, although they have identified a long list of suspects: invasion and draining of wetlands for development, which destroy not only frog habitats but also their vital breeding grounds; the miles of new roads added each year, which invade habitats, bisect frog and toad migration routes, and cause mortality by cars and trucks; large-scale logging, which destroys habitat, particularly in neotropical and tropical forests, areas with the highest diversity of frogs and toads; pollution in the form of pesticides, fertilizers, and toxic chemicals, which results in physical deformities and abnormalities as well as death; diseases and parasites; invasive and introduced predators; changes in the earth's climate and depletion of the ozone layer, which lead to droughts and shifts in weather patterns; increased levels of acid rain, which turn ponds and other water sources into inhospitable frog-breeding environments; and an increase in ultraviolet radiation, which can interfere with development of tadpoles.

Recently a new suspect was discovered, and scientists thought it might provide them with an important clue to the reason for the population declines. This suspect, chytrid fungus, was identified in frogs in 1993, when it was discovered in

populations of the sharp-nosed torrent frog, *Taudactylus acutirostris,* which lives in the rain forests of northern Queensland, Australia.

Chytrid fungi typically occur in water or soil, and several types are known to affect plants and insects, but the discovery of the fungus in the Australian frog was the first time it was found in a vertebrate. When the fungus invades a frog's skin, it damages a substance called keratin, a protein that also forms the basis of human fingernails and hair. Scientists are not sure exactly how the fungus affects the frogs, but the damage to the skin may make it difficult for the animal to absorb oxygen as it normally does, and the frog may suffocate.

Although the fungal disease was reported only in the past decade, herpetologists think that it may have been responsible for amphibian declines dating back to the 1970s and that it has been present in Australia since at least 1978. The fungus also seems to be very widespread; infected frogs have been identified in Australia, Africa, Europe, and South, Central, and North America. Chytrid fungus has probably been spread by people moving from one area to another and introducing frog species into new habitats.

Project Golden Frog

The Panamanian golden frog is considered a national symbol in the Republic of Panama, like the bald eagle in the United States. Thousands of years ago, pre-Columbian cultures crafted gold and clay frogs as talismans. They revered the golden frog and associated it with a sacred site. Anyone seeing or possessing a live frog would have good fortune. Today, you would be hard-pressed to see one of these rare frogs in the wild. What happened to them? As the human population of Panama has grown, new housing developments have been built. One subdivision is right in the middle of existing golden frog habitat. Other areas are being deforested for lumber and cattle ranching, and rock mining for home construction has invaded still more sites. Pesticides and other chemicals used by farmers growing watercress for commercial markets are another threat,

Chytrid fungus was first discovered in the sharp-nosed torrent frog (above), native to Australia. However, the fungus seems to be widespread and has since shown up in frog populations around the world.

The Endangered Panamanian golden frog, *Atelopus zeteki*

as is collection for the pet trade. Added to all these man-made stresses is chytrid fungus, which has been found in a number of the golden frog populations.

Concerned about the future of the Panamanian golden frog, a group of scientists formed Project Golden Frog (*Proyecto Rana Dorada* in Spanish). Small groups of golden frogs were collected in the wild and brought to zoos that belong to the American Zoo and Aquarium Association. More than fifteen North American zoos now participate in the captive-breeding program, and they have produced thousands of golden frogs. Meanwhile, other herpetologists are studying the frogs that remain in the wild and their habitats. They hope to work with biologists in Panama to establish a breeding and education facility in that country, and some day to release captive-bred Panamanian golden frogs into protected areas in their native environment where they have been lost.

Paradise Lost in an Elfin Forest

The worst part of the disappearances is that frogs and toads are vanishing from the most unlikely places—nature reserves, national parks, and extremely remote areas not yet developed by people. All is not well, for example, in Costa Rica's wildlife reserves. More than 40 percent of the frogs and toads, twenty species, in the Monteverde region of the country disappeared or declined during the 1980s. Up until that time, heavy tropical rains deluged the Monteverde Cloud Forest Preserve each year from April through June. The rains formed small temporary pools in the forest, and huge numbers of Monteverde golden toads, *Bufo periglenes,* would gather around these wet places to breed. Competition between males for breeding rights to females was so fierce that the males would form "toad balls," in which four to ten males would clasp each other in amplexus, with an

The Monteverde golden toad disappeared from its cloud forest habitat in Costa Rica during the late 1980s. Males often formed breeding "balls" in which a number of males clasped a female and each other.

unfortunate female toad buried somewhere in the pile.

Also called golden toads because the males are a very striking orange color, these amphibians occupied a small habitat—less than four square miles—of elfin cloud forest between about 6500 and 7000 feet elevation. The forest is called elfin because the understory is filled with mosses, ferns, and epiphytes (air plants that grow on or are in some manner attached to another plant or object for physical support). Year round, this magical forest was covered in a veil of clouds, and the humidity levels measured 100 percent. In this moist, foggy climate, life was perfect for Monteverde toads, until people began cutting the forests at sea level some thirty miles away.

Today, when the trade winds blow over the now barren coast, they pick up less moisture. The hotter and drier air mass must then climb higher up the Tilaran Mountains before there is enough moisture to produce a cloud cover in the Monteverde Preserve. In addition, 1982–83 and 1986–87 were years of the El Niño/Southern Oscillation, a periodic fluctuation in ocean currents that brings warm water to the surface along the west coast of South America. With the addition of the effects of global warming, many scientists believe the golden toads were literally left high and dry in their forest retreat. Less moisture in the region also may have appealed to other frog species and predators that moved into the Monteverde toads' range.

By 1988, only a few years after scientists first reported the toads' mass breeding phenomenon, the toads had virtually disappeared. The following year one adult male was seen. Since then no Monteverde toads have been sighted. Some people are hopeful that the toads are hiding and waiting for good climate conditions to return to their breeding sites, but many experts believe the species is Extinct.

Introduced Predators

Humans have been altering their environments since they first appeared on earth. As people move from one area to another, they often bring animals and plants with them. For example, the European starling was introduced to the United States in the 1800s when one hundred of the birds were released in New York City. Today the birds are widespread in the country. Many plants that are cultivated for gardens also become invasive species when they begin to grow outside the gardens' boundaries.

In 1915 University of California at Berkeley biologist Joseph Grinnell noted that while surveying the wildlife of the Sierra Nevada, his team found so many mountain yellow-legged frogs, *Rana muscosa,* that they were stepping on them. Now there may be only five thousand adult frogs left in fewer than two hundred populations in the species' entire range from north of Lake Tahoe to below Sequoia National Park. In a study published in spring 2004, another U. C. Berkeley researcher, Vance T. Vredenburg, demonstrated that introduced trout are to blame.

The mountain yellow-legged frog lives in cold clear lakes up to twelve thousand feet in altitude. In the 1950s and '60s the California Department of Fish and Game began dumping trout fingerlings from planes into high-Sierra lakes to enhance sport fishing. The fingerlings made short work of frog tadpoles, while the fish proliferated. As part of Vredenburg's study the scientists cleared five lakes in Kings Canyon National Park of trout and then watched the frog populations rebound within three years.

In the case of the mountain yellow-legged frog, the solution to its disappearance is easy: Just get rid of the trout. They are not native to the lakes and are there only for sport fishing. Cane toads, *Bufo marinus,* are a different matter. These large predators, which are prolific breeders, were introduced around the world to eradicate insect pests. They much preferred other prey, however, and in some areas have eaten all the other frog species. By now it would be impossible to eliminate all the introduced populations of cane toads.

Another introduced species, the American bullfrog, which is native to the eastern United States, is now living well and eating native frogs in many western states, Hawaii, Mexico, South American, Europe, Asia, and some of the islands in the Caribbean. Smaller frogs and toads native to these areas are no match for the bigger bullfrogs. And the introduced species may transmit diseases, such as the chytrid fungus, to the native frogs.

We Love Them to Death

Many people like to keep frogs and toads as pets, particularly the brightly colored varieties. Poison frogs, tree frogs, and red tomato frogs are favorites of amphibian hobbyists. But keeping frogs can be a lot of work. Their enclosures and water sources must be kept clean. Many frog species have fairly simple light, temperature, and humidity requirements, but they are very sensitive to contaminants and waste in their environment. Some frogs have specialized diets and nutritional needs, and pet frogs need tending when their caretakers go on vacation.

Some of the smaller, quite active frogs may be fun to watch, but many of the larger frog species are sedentary sit-and-wait predators. They don't move around much. Some people may find these frogs boring after a while and release them into the surrounding countryside, regardless of where they originated. But the local pond or stream may be totally unsuitable to the needs of the frog. On the other hand, some species, like the African clawed frog, *Xenopus laevis,* survive quite well when released into new areas and may compete with native wildlife for habitat and food resources. Released frogs may also introduce new diseases to resident frogs.

Virtual Frogs

Thirty years ago untold numbers of frogs were routinely used in high school biology classes because frogs and humans are both vertebrates and have similar organs and biological systems. In the early 1970s, 13 million northern leopard frogs, *Rana pipiens,* were used in teaching and research. According to commercial trade records, one enterprise collected more than ten tons of frogs from one western state to satisfy market demands. Four years later that same supplier collected only two hundred and fifty pounds from the same area. The wild population simply could not withstand the high level of collecting.

Today some states and countries have banned the commercial harvesting of frogs from the wild for school dissection. Leopard frogs are now bred for laboratory use, and schools have altered their practice of providing a frog for every student, instead assigning a group of students to one frog specimen. And thanks to the Internet, schools can obtain frog-friendly alternatives via online interactive frog dissection programs, such as Net Frog, froguts.com, and the Virtual Frog Dissection Kit.

A Good Project Bad for Frogs

The frogs and other amphibians most likely to be affected by human activities are long-lived species that are slow to reach sexual maturity, those with low reproductive rates, species with poor dispersal and little ability to colonize new areas, and those that are restricted to certain habitats and have special needs. The Kihansi spray toad, *Nectophrynoides asperginis,* is an example of the last type.

According to Isaac Newton's Third Law of Physics, for every action there is an equal and opposite reaction. This was certainly the case in a recent project to improve the lives of people living in southern Tanzania. In November 2000 the World Bank, which finances development projects, contacted the Bronx Zoo and asked its herpetologists to help save the Kihansi spray toad. The only known population of this tiny toad lives in less than two square miles of wetlands that are kept moist by the spray from waterfalls in the Kihansi River. The toad was threatened by the construction of a huge hydroelectric power project that was to provide more electricity for people in cities, but would shut off most of the river flow to the Kihansi Gorge, thus altering the toad's spray-zone habitat. Zoo staff and Tanzanian experts decided to collect some of the wild toads, which were imported into the United States and distributed among the Bronx Zoo and other partner zoos for a captive-breeding program. In addition, a sprinkler system was installed in the gorge to simulate the toad's misty wetland habitat.

The captive-breeding program was extremely successful—more than seven hundred toads were born at the Bronx Zoo alone—but many of the minute, delicate offspring died, and many of the adult founders succumbed to parasites. In addition, the toads were extremely expensive to maintain. Just the cost of the infinitesimally small food items they required was prohibitive. Meanwhile, the wild population was reported to be doing relatively well under the artificial sprinkler system. But because the landscape had changed, predators were moving in and the toads were crowded into a fraction of their former habitat. It appeared to be a blueprint for disaster.

In June 2003 the Tanzanian government released more water from the Kihansi Gorge to see if conditions in the spray toad's habitat would improve without using the sprinklers. Within about a week the estimated population of eighteen thousand toads dropped to just forty. Since then, scientists have discovered that the toads and other amphibians in the region were infected with the chytrid fungus. It is not clear, however, whether the toads' decline was caused by the initial dramatic loss of the spray-zone habitat, contamination of the water supply upstream, increased predation from invading ants and birds, the fungus, or all of these stress factors that combined when humans tampered with the toads' natural environment.

The Kihansi spray toad is presumed to be extinct in the wild. As of early 2005, about one hundred remained in the captive-breeding program.

CHAPTER SEVEN

WHY FROGS ARE IMPORTANT

PEOPLE HAVE BEEN eating frogs for thousands of years, and they are still an important diet component in some parts of the world. Not long ago people in the United States ate frogs regularly. The model for Mark Twain's "Celebrated Jumping Frog of Calaveras County," the California red-legged frog, *Rana aurora draytonii,* was once so abundant that it was a major human food source in the San Francisco Bay area and the Central Valley. During the second half of the nineteenth century thousands of Americans migrated west to California, where gold was supposed to be easy to find but food was scarce and expensive. They hunted wildlife for some of their meals, and consumed about eighty thousand frogs (mostly their legs) annually. The red-legged frog produces many offspring each year, but couldn't withstand such consumption and was nearly driven to extinction. Later incursions by man: logging, wetland draining, cattle grazing, and the like, also affected the frog, and in 1996 it was listed as Threatened under the U.S. Endangered Species Act.

California red-legged frog, *Rana aurora draytonii*

Food for Thought

In the United States frog legs are still considered good to eat; they are carried mainly on menus of fancy restaurants. In 1976 the U.S. imported more than 5.5 million pounds of frog legs, mostly from Japan and India. (In 1987 India banned frog exports after declines in its native frog populations led to an increase in mosquitoes, malaria, and the use of pesticides to control insect numbers.) Annual frog consumption in France has been estimated to be between six and eight million pounds, primarily frogs imported from Bangladesh and Indonesia.

FROGFACT In the early 1900s consumer demand for frog legs was so high in California that American bullfrogs were imported from the East Coast for frog "farming." Bullfrogs, however, are larger than the native California red-legged frogs and are voracious predators. When the farms failed, the remaining bullfrogs easily established themselves in the countryside and either ate the native species or drove them out of their habitats.

Most of the commercial harvest of frogs comes from collecting in the wild, not from frog farms.

More important than providing food for people, frogs form critical links in nature's food chain. They feed on a wide variety of organisms, such as algae, plants, and insects. In turn, many other organisms rely on frogs for their food, including snakes, alligators, and birds. Remove the frogs from any ecosystem, and important links are knocked out of the food chain. Earth's ecological processes are delicately balanced and intricate. Impacts that seem trivial when taken by themselves can become critical when they pile up.

Frogs and Human Health

Frogs may also directly benefit human health. Like humans, frogs contract tuberculosis. By studying the amphibian version of this disease, researchers at Stanford University have identified two genes that may enable the TB bacterium to survive for

Frog Band-Aids

Scientists are exploring naturally occurring animal and plant chemical compounds to find new drugs for human ailments. Frogs are proving to be an important ally in this search. In recent years biologists operating on the African clawed frog, *Xenopus laevis*, noticed that its wounds never became infected. On close examination they discovered that hundreds of white dots appeared on the frog's skin in response to adrenalin being rubbed onto it. Adrenalin is normally released when pain receptors in the skin send a message to the brain that an injury has occurred. The white dots soon merged into a creamy white sheen that covered the skin like a bandage. This "Band-Aid" was filled with bacteria-killing antibiotic peptides, one of which was named magainin, after the Hebrew word *magain*, or "shield." This discovery led to the finding of similar peptide antibiotics in other amphibians, as well as in fish, birds, mammals, and even plants. Discoveries of new antibacterial drugs that are immune to resistance, as well as peptides that are active against disease-causing viruses, fungi, and protozoa, all began with a humble frog.

years within the human body. As with the majority of the two billion humans who contract this disease, most frogs infected with the TB bacterium don't become ill. Instead, they develop a life-long condition in which the bacteria linger within the body without causing symptoms. If the frogs' immune systems are weakened, however, the animals will develop an infection that kills them.

Pain Killer ABT-594

The phantasmal poison frog, *Epipedobates tricolor*, from Ecuador, is one of the most poisonous frogs known to man. Just one carries enough toxins in its skin to take out an entire football team. This toxic compound, called epibatidine in honor of the frog, is remarkably similar to nicotine in structure. An extract from the frog's skin has been found to block pain two hundred times more effectively than morphine. However, potent side effects have limited use of epibatidine in medicine. Researchers at Abbott Laboratories realized its great potential and looked for ways to eliminate the dangerous side effects. Based upon a study of the frog's toxin, they synthesized ABT-594, which appears to be a revolutionary drug for the treatment of pain that carries none of the serious side effects of morphine and is expected to be in use within five to ten years.

The same thing can happen in a TB-infected human whose immune system is then attacked by a virus or other disease. The findings in frogs may help clear up the mystery of how the TB bacterium establishes itself within the very immune system cells that are supposed to destroy it.

In other research, scientists at Cambridge University in England have been working with immature *Xenopus* frog eggs to rejuvenate adult human cells. Molecules in the amphibian cell nucleus have been shown to reprogram human DNA to an immature stem cell-like state. The researchers hope to isolate the substances in the frog cells responsible for the reprogramming and use them to create immature human cells.

Human stem cells derived from early-stage human embryos have been used to repair tissue damaged by diseases such as Parkinson's and multiple sclerosis. But the use of human embryos has caused ethical dilemmas. Employing frog eggs to create cells resembling stem cells could bypass the ethical and practical problems of human stem cell research.

And let's not forget that each year frogs eat billions of insects, many of which carry diseases that affect people. According to some experts, a single African dwarf puddle frog, *Phrynobatrachus,* can eat up to one hundred mosquitoes in a night. The penchant that frogs and toads have for insects also saves the spending of untold millions of dollars on pesticides by the agriculture industry. Frogs and toads are free bug zappers, and they work much better than the electrical kind.

Conserving Frogs

Frogs have been on earth for millions of years, outliving dinosaurs and many other animals that once roamed our planet. The secret to their success is their amazing adaptability. Yet, the adaptive qualities of frogs are not inexhaustible. They can be defeated, as we have seen. And the loss of frogs could have serious consequences for man.

Frogs and toads are indicators, like the canaries that coal miners once carried into the mines to make sure the air was safe for people to breathe. If conditions in earth's natural environments are adversely affecting frogs and toads worldwide, it does not bode well for the other beings that share this small planet. For this reason, if no other, mankind would do well to look out for its frogs.

In 1997, a group of herpetologists formed the Amphibian Conservation Alliance, a nonprofit environmental organization, to provide a database of resources and information. In 1998 federal agencies in the United States formed the Taskforce on Amphibian Declines and Deformities, with four working groups focusing on international, science, conservation, and education activities. That same year Partners in Amphibian and Reptile Conservation was established to improve communication and cooperation among government agencies, industries, education and funding institutions, and the public. And in the summer of 2000 the U.S. Fish and Wildlife Service launched a study of wildlife refuges to investigate why amphibians are disappearing in protected areas and the causes of deformities in frogs, toads, and salamanders.

Paramount to any conservation effort is to identify and deal with the reasons species are in danger of extinction. Since the alarming reports of frog deformities and disappearances surfaced in the late 1980s, many experts in a variety of fields have mobilized to study the problem. The first of these international investigatory teams, the Declining Amphibian Populations Task Force (DAPTF), was formed in 1990, operating under the umbrella of the World Conservation Union. Thousands of scientists across geographic regions have joined working groups to coordinate their studies of potential causes of amphibian declines. The DAPTF produces "Froglog," a newsletter updating recent findings.

Good News

The harlequin, or clown frog, *Atelopus varius,* once lived along forest streams in Colombia, Panama, and Costa Rica. During the dry season the frogs would congregate in the splash zones of these watercourses. Then in the late 1980s scientists began to note that the numbers of this species

Harlequin frog, *Atelopus varius*

of harlequin frog were dropping dramatically. In Costa Rica, particularly in the Monteverde region, the species really crashed; it was last sighted there in 1996. Experts believe climate change, habitat loss, and pathogens such as the chytrid fungus may have caused the toad's disappearance. In 2003, however, a local guide with the Rainmaker Conservation Project discovered a population of clown frogs in the Fila Chonta mountain range in southwest Costa Rica. The Atlanta Botanical Garden, in Georgia, is leading a harlequin frog conservation and captive-breeding effort to help protect this newly discovered population and ensure the species' survival in the wild. There were more than seventy-five species of harlequin frogs in the *Atelopus* genus in Central and South America. Scientists believe that more than half of these have become extinct in recent years.

Test Tube Amphibians

In July 2004 the Memphis Zoo announced that it had produced the world's first endangered amphibians through artificial fertilization. While researchers have been performing artificial fertilization on amphibian eggs for more than thirty years, this is the first time that an endangered amphibian species—in this case, the Wyoming toad, *Bufo baxteri*—has benefited from this technology.

The Wyoming toad was once abundant in wetlands and irrigated meadows in the southeastern plains of that state's Laramie River basin. In the mid- to late 1970s the toad suddenly became scarce. Biologists have speculated that predators and chytrid fungus are at least partially to blame. At the same time, the region's populations of the northern leopard frog, *Rana pipiens,* became Extinct. One small group of Wyoming toads was found at Mortenson Lake, twenty miles west of Laramie. In 1988 the handful of breeding adult pairs were caught and placed in a captive breeding program, and the federal government launched the Wyoming Toad Recovery Plan. The Nature Conservancy bought the lake and the surrounding lands, and the federal government purchased

some of that land for the Mortenson Lake National Wildlife Refuge. Nevertheless, by 1994, the Wyoming toad was declared Extinct in the wild.

Since then, breeding programs by the Wyoming Game and Fish Department and a number of North American zoos have produced thousands of eggs and young. Some of the tadpoles and toadlets are retained for the breeding programs, which have about six hundred frogs, and the rest, more than ten thousand, have been released into protected areas of the wild habitat. To date, however, only a small number of adult toads have survived.

The artificial fertilization technology employed by Memphis Zoo biologists will help improve the genetic diversity among the captive and wild populations of Wyoming toads, and it enabled the Memphis Zoo to produce and send to the wild more than 1700 Wyoming toad tadpoles. The scientists hope this technology will help in the recovery of other Critically Endangered frog and toad species.

What You Can Do

It has become increasingly clear that, though the experts are on the case, there will be no smoking gun to explain the large number of frog disappearances and declines. In most instances, there isn't a single cause. Rather, it is a combination of factors that spell doom for these curious and fascinating little animals.

And it isn't only the amphibians that will suffer. Without frogs and toads, we will be overrun with mosquitoes and other harmful pests. Many larger animals, like snakes, fish, herons, and other waterbirds that depend on amphibians for food, will disappear. To quote Kermit the Frog, "If you wait until the frogs and toads have croaked their last to take some action, you've missed the point."

There are things you can do every day to help make the planet a better place to live for both frogs and people.

❏ Homeowners should choose nonchemical weed controls wherever possible, limit the use of fertilizers, and reduce dependence on pesticides. Chemicals can wash into streams and lakes, harming or killing frogs.

❏ When you are hiking, take pictures and memories, not souvenirs. Carry binoculars, a camera, and a notebook to keep track of the plants and animals you see. But leave these wild species where they belong, in their native habitat.

❏ When you drive, go slow when frogs in your area are breeding. Many frogs and other amphibians get run over as they migrate to their breeding ponds and pools.

❏ Properly dispose of paint, oil, and other hazardous wastes. Don't dump them down the drain. Not only can they pollute your drinking water, but they also wash into streams and lakes where frogs live and breed.

❏ If you think you want a frog as a pet, do prior research to decide on the type of frog that best suits your needs and to learn how to care for it.

❏ Don't release unwanted pet fish, turtles, or frogs into a pond. They might carry disease or may prey on native species.

❏ Help experts in your area carry out a frog census.

❏ Support organizations and laws that champion the preservation of amphibians and their habitats.

Frog-logging

For more than a hundred years bird experts and amateur bird watchers have conducted organized counts to monitor the status and distribution of bird populations across the Western Hemisphere. In 2003 more than fifty thousand volunteers joined in over 1800 counts of bird species and numbers. It's not difficult; all you need is a pair of binoculars, a good field guide to birds, and a working knowledge of various bird songs.

What has this got to do with frogs? Well, herpetologists concerned about disappearing and deformed frogs and toads decided that citizen science is a good thing. In 1994 they decided to mimic the success of the bird counts and launched the U.S. Geological Survey's North American Amphibian Monitoring Program (NAAMP).

Through NAAMP, volunteer observers are recruited and trained by regional coordinators to collect information about amphibian populations. The observers collect data using what is known as a calling survey technique. First, volunteers are trained to identify the vocalizations of local frogs and toads in their region. Then, each year during the amphibian breeding season, in both the United States and Canada, participants drive along routes that have been established by the U.S. Geological Survey's Patuxent Wildlife Research Center and stop at potential wetland amphibian breeding sites. There they listen for calling frogs and toads, and record the data they gather. The routes average fifteen miles long, and each survey route has ten listening stations. Surveys are conducted in the evening, when most amphibians are active, and the routes are surveyed three to four times a year, because different species breed at different times.

This is an activity the whole family can enjoy, and the volunteer "amphibian army" provides a vital service to scientists and others trying to protect these vulnerable animals. For more information about how you can become a frog-logger, visit the NAAMP website at http://www.pwrc.usgs.gov/naamp/, or contact them by telephone at (301) 497-5500.

CHAPTER EIGHT

GETTING THE PICTURE

THE LITTLE BUGGER HAS VANISHED! Gone!! You'll hear these words often, or something similar, from photographers who stalk wild frogs for fun or profit. Capturing great images of frogs in nature can be extremely difficult. Patience, as they say, is a virtue.

Frog photography is in the realm of close-up photography. When taken by a skilled photographer, the magnified images that the camera records reveal the hidden beauty of the frog or toad and expose its intricate features from nose to toes. The frozen details captured in photographs often offer perspectives about frogs that are impossible to see with the naked eye.

Stalking frogs and capturing the perfect image—like this green frog in flight— takes practice, patience, the proper photo equipment, and often many exposures.

The art and science of photography is about understanding how your camera works, how it "sees," and directing its vision to meet your needs. If the photographer does not have a vision of what he or she wants to achieve in the image, and the knowledge to fulfill that objective, the results will disappoint. Most of the time poor photos are not due to camera failure, but to the fault of the user. Professional photographers or not, those who take the best photos are skilled at seizing the photographic moment and can quickly compose and set up the shot so that the final image closely resembles what they perceived in their mind's eye.

To become an accomplished frog photographer, you will need the photographic equipment that matches your interests and skills, as well as the field attire and related gear that allow you to enter their world. But before you get started photographing wildlife, you will need to know something about your quarry: the species' habitat, what time of the day it is active, and what period of its natural cycle provides the best opportunity for capturing excellent shots.

In addition to these basic requirements, your ears and eyes are the best tools. But they too need training. Whether in the field during the day or at night, *walk slowly* in wetlands, through a wet meadow, or along a woodland trail. *Stop frequently* and survey the terrain around you. Let your eyes explore the ground and pockets of water, as well as the tree trunks, vines, and leaves of shrubs. What well-camouflaged creature is quietly watching you or making a silent exit from the scene? Look carefully for subtle movements made by animals in response to those made by you. Listen for calling frogs in the distance and the rustle of leaves nearby.

A frog's breeding season is the ideal time to take memorable photographs. If you are after images of wood frogs, for example, the best place to look for this species is at vernal ponds, at night in March, often before the first days of spring arrive. There you will also find spring peepers and spotted salamanders as well as the wood frogs. The frogs' unique voices and loud choruses, which sometimes can be heard from a half mile away, give them away. Gray tree frogs often use the same ponds, but you will not hear their voices on a March night. You'll have to wait until a warm May evening for them to arrive.

In addition to its distinctive call, each frog species has a specific calling site. Once you have found one calling male, study the area carefully. Look for other perching situations that appear similar, and you'll find other frogs of the same kind.

In North America, bullfrogs and green frogs—or other frogs and toads that are active during the day—are the best subjects for the budding anuran photographer. In late spring and summer these frogs are frequently found along the edges of permanent ponds and lakes. These sit-and-wait predators allow the frog stalker to develop a "search image" for the quarry and learn how close to approach before the frogs jump to safety.

Field Gear

When searching for frogs during the day, it is best to keep the sun at your back—for the sake of both getting good shots as well as seeing the sun's reflection off your quarry at a distance. Take along a small pair of good lightweight binoculars—perhaps 7 x 36 power. They are helpful for scanning banks, water edges, and weedy shallows for all manner of photographable subjects. Binoculars give the "hunter" the advantage of seeing the animal before it sees him or her, and allow the observer to plan a cautious approach.

Binoculars are an important investment. Models that can focus on subjects as close as four to five feet, as well as long range, are best, because their versatility allows the naturalist to identify species and study their behaviors at a distance or at very close range. They also meet the needs of most butterfly- and birdwatchers.

So what does the well-dressed frog stalker wear, and how is he or she equipped? If you've chosen a 40° night in March, you will need to wear a good pair of hip boots, perhaps ones that are insulated. Although the night may be cold, it is best to dress lightly and in layers to be agile when searching frog haunts. The latest generation of thin thermal underwear, coupled with a polar fleece shirt and vest, thin polypropylene gloves, and a hat will keep you warm. On the other hand, in warm weather or in tropical climates, it's best to abandon the hip boots. Old pants, a long-sleeved shirt for protection against biting insects at night or the sun by day, old sneakers, and a hat are good choices. If you don't like the thought of spending hours in wet sneakers, a well-fitting pair of knee-high dairyman's or gum boots will serve you well.

Many wildlife photographers wear a special vest that holds their notepads, film, lens filters, recording instruments, and assorted gizmos, as well as a fanny pack for an additional camera lens or two. At night a strong, adjustable, tilting headlamp or miners' lamp with long-lasting batteries, such as those sold by popular outdoor equipment companies, is must-have equipment for the field explorer. A headlamp frees your hands, and with the source of light so near your eyes, you will be able to see the reflected eye-shine of frogs, spiders, snakes, alligators, nighthawks, and mammals around you—often from a great distance. In addition, the reflected light from the skin of a wet frog or a sleeping lizard will stand out against its background. But don't forget a small hand-held flashlight as an important backup light source.

Going Digital?

The world of photography is changing rapidly, propelled by the arrival of digital imaging. Although there are ongoing arguments for and against digital cameras, few professional wildlife photographers would disagree that digital photography is rapidly replacing the basic tool of their trade: the 35-mm single-lens reflex (SLR) camera. While digital photography is part of the technology wave of this new century, SLR film cameras recorded nearly all of the photographs in this book. Many of the photographs by John Netherton were taken with a lightweight Nikon N90 or a Nikon F4, coupled to a 60-mm Nikkor macro lens for close work or a 200-mm Nikkor macro lens when he worked farther away from his subject. Netherton used a Nikon SB-21 macro speedlight (ring light, or ring flash) with the 60-mm lens, and two SB-24 Nikon flash units mounted on either side of a flash bracket with the 200-mm lens.

Photographic equipment is evolving quickly, and it's easy to become seduced by the new bells and whistles. Popular articles in photography magazines may convince you that five-year-old 35-mm SLR cameras are obsolete, passé. Not true. In the right hands your father's SLR still takes photographs that compare with the best SLR cameras available today.

You will also see debates on film versus digital photographs. Those who champion digital imaging may think that film cameras are dinosaurs. Both systems have their strengths and weaknesses. When large fine-art photographs are the objective, the SLR camera wins. These cameras capture more information on film than their digital counterparts and are capable of producing larger prints of finer detail and richer tones. For smaller enlargements the quality gap between film and digital cameras has closed. The number of published wildlife photos taken by digital photographers is rapidly climbing. Today many book and magazine designers prefer digital camera images over slide film because they save them the time and money they would have to spend to have the slides professionally digitized to meet their standards.

For less demanding photographers small point-and-shoot digital cameras offer a wealth of photographic tools, such as advanced metering, that are not found on comparably sized point-and-shoot film cameras. Captured digital images may be viewed immediately, and the photographer can make adjustments if they are required. Debate continues about the pluses and minuses of computer processing and image enhancement. For both, better methods will continue to evolve.

Which camera is right for you depends upon your particular needs. If you are a herpetologist and want stop-action photographs of a frog sticking out its tongue or parachuting, you will require a top-notch camera with high-speed strobe lights. This is very specialized photography. Most people's needs are simpler. For example, biologists working in the field take photographs to document the species they have found, their behaviors, and habitats. These images will support their field notes and provide an added dimension for their reports, scientific publications, and presentations to both scientific and general audiences.

If you are spending hours in the field, camera weight is a factor to consider. Expensive single-lens reflex cameras, film or digital, are heavy to carry, even in a backpack, and many a photographic opportunity can be lost in the process of setting up the camera. In most situations the field biologist's choice of camera will be much the same as that used by most people for recording general family events: a compact, point-and-shoot digital camera. These cameras are small enough to fit in a large pocket, can be ready in an instant, and have the best ratio of features and performance to price. Current models have sensors able to record in the 3–5 megapixel (the higher the number of pixels, the better) range, a 3 to 4x zoom lens (in the 35–140-mm range), and a variety of exposure modes from full auto to full manual override. Excellent images from these cameras are also publishable as small enlargements. If your purposes for carrying a camera in the field are simply to record your adventures and wildlife encounters to share with friends, seriously consider the compact digital camera as an initial low-cost investment.

If you decide that you need a 35-mm SLR camera or its digital SLR (DSLR) counterpart, Nikon and Canon cameras with autofocusing and automatic settings are the choice of many photographers. Although other brands of single-lens reflex cameras are excellent, they are less popular because they lack extensive support systems, including a wide assortment of lenses and flash accessories. Because some people get hung up on the equipment rather than the photographs they take, they "trade up" with great regularity. This means that excellent used manual and automatic SLR cameras are often available at greatly reduced prices. While some terrific used high-end manual SLR cameras can be bought at a fraction of their original cost, they do require two hands to operate—one to hold the camera, the second to turn the lens barrel to focus. The auto-focusing feature isn't a necessity, but it is a great help when you are shooting small wildlife under difficult conditions. This feature probably allows more accurate focusing than can be done manually, and it frees a hand to hold a small flashlight on the subject, to help you crawl on the ground toward it, or to support you when you are in a contorted position and a fleeing frog lands on your eyeglasses.

Tripods and Lenses

While you'll find the same basic photographic gear in the equipment bag of the small-animal wildlife photographer and those that pursue birds and large mammals, there is a fundamental difference in their art: telephoto versus close-up photography. In the field the orientation of the photographers can usually be recognized by the size of their camera lens. Most often, bird and mammal photographers must use a telephoto lens, 200–500 mm or larger in size, to fill a frame with the image they desire. Since their subjects are often beyond the range of the light produced by flash units, they must work under natural light conditions and use a tripod. The camera of the amphibian, reptile, and insect photographer is usually equipped with a macro lens coupled to a

flash unit. A compact 100-mm macro lens is often a very popular choice. It allows the photographer to get close enough to the subject to fill the frame without spooking the animal.

Small-animal photographers, however, are often compromised by low light conditions. Under natural lighting conditions, the exposures must often be long and there is little depth of field. In any photograph there is a range of distance over which the subject appears in sharp focus. Without flash the apparent sharpness field is narrow. In low light if you focus on a frog's eye, his nose and toes will likely be out of focus. And natural lighting can be uneven, with the animal's body casting strong shadows.

Because of the slow speed required to take a picture under naturally lighted conditions, it may be impossible to hold the camera still enough to prevent blurring. A tripod will solve this difficulty. For SLR cameras with the now standard through-the-lens light metering (TTL) systems and TTL flash synchronization at up to 1/250 second, these problems are easily corrected by using a compatible flash attachment.

Flash!

Although some nature photographers reject the use of an electronic flash because the light is artificial, most close-up photo specialists find a flash unit to be indispensable for their work. At night there is no option. During the day there are many benefits of flash photography. Very often small animals photographed without a flash simply look lifeless and poorly lighted. Besides allowing increased depth of field, the extra light of a flash eliminates strong contrast and brightens shadowy areas. Of great importance, the light reflected off the animal's eye makes the subject seem to be alive in the photo.

There are many flash attachment choices— from commonly used top-mounted units to extravagant bracket models that support multiple flash units and ring lights. Each has merits, and each has limitations. Multiple flash units set on either side of the flash bracket are terrific for balancing light on the subject and eliminating excessive reflections and shadows that may be a problem with other types of units. Yet they are heavy and cumbersome in the field and best left for staged photographs at home. For many applications top-mounted flash units, especially those that can be tilted toward the subject, work well. They are powerful and are best for subjects that aren't close to the camera. If the animal is close, say a foot or less from the camera, the light from the top-mounted flash may overshoot it or light only its top half.

For these kinds of situations the ring flash has become very popular. These flash units are rather compact and fit around the barrel of the macro lens. The advantages are that the light source is near the subject, allows a small aperture and better depth of field, and is always aimed properly. However, because photos taken with a ring flash are evenly lighted, they may appear flat or less interesting than those taken with multiple flash units. A clear disadvantage is that the light source is comparatively weak, thus limiting the ring flash's application to close macro-photography. Whatever your choice, a flash unit that has a focus illuminator is very helpful, as it offers a source of light for focusing on the subject at night.

If you invest in an expensive top-of-the-line 35-mm camera to take wildlife portraits, you should also invest in film that will yield truly sharp and color saturated images. In general, slower speed films, like ISO 25 to 100, take sharper pictures than fast film, like ISO 200 to 400. The advantage of slower film is that the photographs can be greatly enlarged and still be sharp, while at the same enlargement fast film photos may appear grainy. For macro-photography the use of slow film requires flash, while long-lens wildlife photographers, working in lower light conditions, need fast film where subjects are beyond the effective range of a flash unit. Nearly all the photographs in this book were taken with slow films.

Patience and Practice

Complete mastery of the skills needed to take really fantastic wildlife photographs may take years, but technically proficient shots can come more quickly. Digital photography has reduced the trial-and-error learning curve due to its instant feedback and opportunity for correction. Lens autofocus and vibration reduction features also have helped.

Whether you use film or digital photography to capture your images, the learning process takes time and patience. If your pictures are less than you expect and you ask the experts what to do, they'll likely reply, "Take more pictures." Take notes. Learn what works and what does not. You can also immerse yourself in the process. Well-known wildlife photographers often lead several photo safaris each year. There are specialized trips for those interested in virtually every wildlife photo subject, from insects to elephants, and desert landscapes to rain forests. Their advertisements appear in natural history and wildlife photograph journals. Before you sign up, be completely familiar with your camera and read a good book on wildlife photography. Several are listed under "Further Reading."

Photo Etiquette

If you are shooting with a group of photographers, remember that there is such a thing as photo etiquette. Be considerate of others. When someone discovers something interesting to photograph, be mindful of the fact that a crush of people surrounding a frog on a leaf will certainly scare the animal away. And then the opportunity for a few people to get good photographs is lost.

Ask the leader to set the ground rules for taking photographs. He or she is likely versed in handling these matters, but the rules should be discussed before the day begins. If possible, it is best for everyone in the party to get a look at the animal before taking photographs of it; then "insurance shots" may be taken, followed by orderly close-ups. Remember that the cumulative effects of flash bombardment can take a toll. The animal may leave the security of its retreat to escape the human incursion, thereby exposing itself to predators.

The one rule of wildlife photography that stands above all others is "Do no harm." Never destroy an animal's habitat or hurt the subject you are trying to preserve for the sake of a photo. Some environments are extremely fragile, and trampled habitat may not recover for a decade or more.

There is also debate about the virtues of staging photographs. They range from the never-do-it camps to those who stage all their photographs in the studio in miniature habitat replicas. The frog photographs in this book are from all areas of the spectrum. Some are taken in nature exactly as the frogs and toads were encountered, others were turned or moved a few feet to make the shot better. Some are captive-bred specimens, and others are wild-caught individuals that were photographed in setups and later released where they were captured. For many naturalists the thrill of the shot is getting it in nature, exactly as the subject was found. In many ways these kinds of photos, even though they are not as sharp as a tack or perfectly exposed, have more scientific merit than do staged photos, since they are recordings of real-life events. Nevertheless, it is sometimes impossible to capture certain scientific or aesthetic aspects of a small animal without staging it. Special care should be taken to avoid injuring the subject when capturing it and returning it to the site where it was discovered. The time between capture and release should be as brief as possible. For amphibians that have narrow temperature requirements and can dehydrate quickly, it is especially important that they be kept moist and not exposed to high temperatures. No photograph should ever be taken at the expense of the well-being of the subject.

Beginner's Tips

You have purchased your camera and are set for an adventure capturing images of frogs or other wildlife. The following tips may help make your first outing a success. Good shooting.

1. Carefully read the camera manual and the camera tips information that come with your purchase.

2. Take a dealer-sponsored workshop on how to get the best results from your camera.

3. Learn from others. Most wildlife photographers are pleased to be asked about how they get good pictures. Read wildlife photography journals and note the technical information that accompanies great photos—the exposure time, aperture, and film speed. If you want to specialize in photographing amphibians and reptiles, read a book by photographers who specialize in that subject, such as *How to Photograph Reptiles and Amphibians,* by L. West and W. P. Leonard, 1997.

4. Focus your creative energies on taking good pictures in the field, rather than the hike itself. Try to anticipate the shots that you'll be taking and plan carefully for the opportunity when it presents itself.

Start by finding a few good wildlife locations near your home and become intimately familiar with them, the wildlife they support, their habitats, and where the best opportunities for getting well-composed photographs are located. Select spots where you can hide and watch wildlife behaviors. Pond and lake edges are good places to see amphibians and reptiles.

5. Provide a good foundation for your camera. For sit-and-wait photography during the day, a tripod may make a big difference. It is essential for telephoto lenses. If your camera is not steady, you will not get sharp results. Learn to hold your camera properly. If you are right-handed, rest your camera in your left hand, and if you have a single-lens reflex camera, place your left hand under the lens. Your elbows should be held close to your sides and your camera pressed close to your forehead when you look through the viewfinder. In effect, this forms a tripod and steadies the camera. If necessary, lean against a tree or solid object or sit down and brace your elbows on your legs. A bean bag is also helpful in providing a steady rest. Gently press the shutter release—roll your finger over it, do not jerk it.

6. Be mindful of the location of the sun. Experienced wildlife photographers generally avoid taking photos at midday on bright sunny days, because the light conditions are fierce and the photographic results are generally poor. In the morning face west, and in the afternoon face east, as it will keep the sunlight from coming into your lens and washing out your photographs.

7. A well-composed photo tells us more about wildlife than a simple portrait. Putting every subject in the middle of the photograph becomes boring. Generally, it is important to keep the whole animal in the photograph, but compose carefully so that the background tells a story. Behavioral images are difficult to capture. Learn to anticipate them and be ready to take advantage of them.

8. Always try to be on or close to the same level as the subject you are photographing. Animals, just like people, look much better when you are even with the subject. Let the animals enter your world. For a portrait, animals quartering toward you look better than in sideways mug shots.

9. Approach your subject carefully. No jerky movements. Move slowly but steadily and avoid eye contact or prematurely pointing the camera at the subject. The lens may look like a big preda-

tor's eye. Try not to let your shadow fall on the animal. Take an insurance shot when the first opportunity presents itself.

10. Some animals, including frogs, are fragile creatures. The nicotine-coated fingers of a heavy smoker may kill a frog with a touch. Wear latex gloves if these photo subjects must be handled and change them when the photo subject changes. Some frogs are quite toxic to others, so for safety's sake different species should not be confined together.

11. Take lots of pictures! Bracket your photos for insurance by keeping the camera speed constant and changing the aperture setting one-half to one f-stop above and below the automatic setting indicated. For example, if the automatic setting indicates 1/125 of a second at f11, take photos at that setting as well as photos at 1/125 of a second at f8 and f16. Take notes. Learn what works, what does not. There are great photographic opportunities available each day. When you discover them, don't snap a shot or two and exclaim, "I've got it!" You may have gotten the best shot that the opportunity presented, but probably not. As long as the frog is there, stick with it and take additional shots so that you can learn from your failures and successes.

GLOSSARY

Adaptation In biology, a process by which an animal or plant becomes fitted to its environment; a feature that particularly suits the lifestyle of an organism or a group of related organisms.

Advertisement call A sound produced by a male frog to establish his territory or to attract females to the breeding site, and, in some cases, to deter rival males.

Aestivation A state of inactivity during prolonged periods of drought or high temperatures.

Aggregation A group or mass consisting of many individuals, as in a breeding aggregation.

Alkaloids A group of chemical compounds in some plants and animals; of great importance because of their poisonous and medicinal properties.

Amphibian A vertebrate animal with a soft, scaleless outer skin that spends part of its life on land and part in the water. Frogs and toads are amphibians.

Amplexus An embrace, adopted during mating in most species of frogs, in which the male clasps the female with its forelimbs and/or hind limbs.

Anuran A member of the order Anura, frogs and toads.

Aquatic Frequenting or living in water.

Arboreal Tree dwelling.

Barbel A long, slender, fleshy feeler on the chin of an aquatic tadpole.

Batesian mimicry A form of biological resemblance in which a noxious, or dangerous, organism, equipped with a warning system such as conspicuous coloration, is mimicked by a harmless organism.

Bromeliad A flowering plant that lives attached to a larger plant.

Caecilian A legless burrowing tropical amphibian resembling a worm.

Carnivore An animal that eats the flesh of other animals.

Casque A helmetlike modification of the skull.

Chromatophore A special cell containing pigment, usually located in the outer layers of skin.

Cilia Hairlike structures.

Class A taxonomic category ranking that comes below kingdom and above the order (example: frogs and toads are in the class Amphibia).

Cloaca A single cavity, or chamber, in the bodies vent of amphibians into which urinary, digestive, and reproductive systems empty.

Cloud forest A moist, high-altitude forest characterized by dense undergrowth, ferns, mosses, and other plants growing on the trunks and branches of trees.

Clutch A group of eggs.

Convergent evolution A process whereby unrelated species living in similar but separate physical environments are shaped by natural selection to have comparable morphological, physiological, or life history characteristics.

Cryptic Hidden, or camouflaged; difficult to see.

Desiccation The process of drying out.

Dimorphism Difference in form, color, or structure in members of the same species.

Direct development The transition from the egg to the adult form in amphibians without passing through a free-living tadpole stage.

Diurnal Active during the day.

Dormant Inactive.

Dorsal Pertaining to the back or the upper surface of the body.

Ectotherm A cold-blooded animal; it cannot regulate its body temperature internally and relies on external heat sources to do so. Frogs and toads are ectotherms.

Egg A female gamete or ovum and the surrounding membranes.

Encounter call A call made by a male frog or toad when a rival male approaches or calls from nearby.

Endotherm A warm-blooded animal that regulates its body temperature using its own internal heat. Mammals and birds are endotherms.

Environment The complex of physical, chemical, and biological factors that acts upon an organism or an ecological community and ultimately determines its form and survival.

Epidermis The surface layer of the skin of a vertebrate.

Estivation A state of inactivity and seclusion to avoid periods of high temperature and drought.

Evolution A process in which a population of organisms, molded by environmental changes, gradually alters its characteristics over a long period of time.

Explosive breeder A species in which the breeding season is very short, resulting in large numbers of frogs coming together and mating at the same time.

External fertilization Fusing of eggs and sperm outside the female's body.

Family A taxonomic category ranking that comes below the order and above the genus (example: family Ranidae (true frogs), family Hylidae (tree frogs).

Fertilization The union of egg and sperm.

Food pyramid A series of inter-connected feeding relationships called food chains. Most food chains consist of three or four levels. A typical sequence may be plant, herbivore, carnivore, top carnivore.

Fossil The remains, impression, cast, or trace of an animal or plant of a past geological period, preserved in rock.

Froglet A newly metamorphosed juvenile frog that is a small replica of the adult.

Genus (plural **genera**) A taxo-nomic category that contains one or more species and ranks below family and above species; the first word in the scientific name of a species. Example: *Hyla* in the species name *Hyla gratiosa*.

Geological period The basic unit of the geologic timescale. During these spans of time, specific systems of rocks were formed.

Gill A respiratory structure in the tadpole stage through which oxygen and carbon dioxide are exchanged.

Gland A cell or organ that produces one or more chemical compounds, which are passed to the outside of the gland.

Global warming Increase in global average surface temperatures.

Gravid Carrying eggs or young.

Habitat The environment or type of conditions in which an animal lives.

Herbivore An animal that eats plants.

Herpetology The study of amphibians and reptiles; biologists who study these animals are called herpetologists.

Hibernation A period of inactivity or dormant state of an animal during cold winter months.

Home range The area in which an animal usually carries out its daily activities, such as sleeping, eating, basking, and reproducing.

Hylid A member of the tree frog family, *Hylidae*.

Internal fertilization Fusing of eggs and sperm inside the female's body.

Introduced A species that is brought from lands where it occurs naturally to regions where it has not previously occurred.

Invertebrate An animal that lacks a backbone.

Iridophore A cell containing white or silvery reflecting platelets.

Jacobson's organ A sensory organ that amphibians and reptiles use to analyze, or "smell," small molecules in the air.

Keratin A tough protein material found in the skin of frogs and toads and in feathers, scales, and human nails and hair.

Larva The preadult form, in which some animals hatch from the egg, capable of fending for themselves. Example: tadpole.

Larynx The modified upper parts of the windpipe; in many vertebrates it contains the vocal chords.

Lateral line organs A system of sense organs over the head and body of tadpoles and aquatic amphibians, which are sensitive to water pressure and currents.

Leptodactylid A member of the southern frog family, Leptodactylidae.

Life cycle The series of changes that the members of a species undergo as they pass from the beginning of a given developmental stage to the inception of that same developmental stage in a subsequent generation, from egg to larva to adult to egg, for example.

Macrophagous Eats large objects.

Melanophore A chromatophore cell with melanin, a dark brown to black pigment.

Metamorphosis The transformation of an animal from one stage of its life to another; in frogs, from the larval or tadpole stage to the juvenile stage, which resembles the adult in form.

Microphagous Eats small objects.

Mimic A harmless, less toxic, or less dangerous species that resembles a toxic or dangerous one.

Molt To shed and develop a new outer covering of the body; in frogs, the shedding of the skin.

Montane Pertaining to mountains.

Mucus The slimy substance that lubricates and moistens the skin of frogs.

Müllerian mimicry A form of biological resemblance in which a noxious or dangerous organism equipped with a warning system such as conspicuous coloration is mimicked by a less toxic or less dangerous species.

Newt A small, semiaquatic salamander.

Nictitating membrane The "third eyelid"; a thin, transparent fold of skin at the inner angle of the eye or below the lower eyelid that can be drawn across the eyeball for protection without obscuring vision.

Nocturnal Active at night.

Nuptial pad A thick, roughened pad on the thumb of a sexually active male frog or toad that helps him hold the female during amplexus.

Omnivore An animal that eats plants and the flesh of other animals.

Oral disc The fleshy parts surrounding a tadpole's mouth.

Order The taxonomic category ranking above family. Examples: order Anura (frogs and toads); order Caudata (salamanders).

Pangaea The earth's single supercontinent that began to fragment about 200 million years ago; continental drift produced the arrangement of the continents we see today.

Parotoid gland One of a pair of swollen glands behind the eye and on the neck of an amphibian; especially prominent on true toads.

Parthenogenesis Reproduction without fertilization by male sperm.

Population A more or less separate group of animals of the same species.

Predator An animal that feeds by hunting and killing other animals.

Ranid A member of the true frog family, Ranidae.

Salamander A four-legged amphibian with a well-defined tail.

Sarcopterygian A group of ancient fish that had lobed fins; one of the first animals to venture out on land.

Satellite male In frogs, a male that does not call himself, but sits near a calling male and intercepts females that are attracted to the calling male.

Seat-patch An area of skin surrounding the vent of a frog or toad; it is often more darkly colored than the rest of the skin. It is the point of body contact of a sitting anuran and may function in fluid uptake.

Shedding Loss of the outer, dead layer of the skin's epidermis.

Siblings Offspring of the same parents; brothers and sisters.

Species The second word in the scientific name of a species. Example: *gratiosa* in the species name *Hyla gratiosa*. A group of interbreeding populations of organisms that are reproductively isolated from other such groups.

Sperm Small, motile male gametes.

Tadpole The larva of a frog or toad.

Taxonomy The science of arranging animals and plants into groups based on their natural relationships, resemblances, and differences.

Temperate zone An area of earth characterized by moderate climate.

Terrestrial Living on land.

Territory An area that one or more animals defend against other members of the same species.

Tetrapod An animal with two pairs of functional limbs.

Toadlet A newly metamorphosed juvenile toad that is a small replica of the adult.

Tubercle A small, knoblike projection.

Tympanum The eardrum; the membrane covering the external opening of the middle ear.

Unken reflex A defensive posture shown by some frogs and other amphibians when attacked; the body is arched inward with the head and tail lifted upward.

Vent An opening from the body; in frogs, the anal opening, or cloaca, to the cloacal chamber.

Ventral Pertaining to the lower surface of the body or other structure.

Vertebrate An animal that has a backbone.

Vocal chords Paired thickenings in the wall of the larynx in a frog or toad that produce vibrations when air from the lungs passes over them.

Vocal sac An expandable pouch on the floor of the mouth and throat of many male frogs and toads that becomes filled with air and acts as a resonating chamber when the animal vocalizes during courtship.

Warning coloration Bright (often red, orange, yellow against black) markings on an animal that is distasteful or poisonous, advertising this condition to predators. Warning coloration is presumed to aid predators' learning to stay away.

Wart A rounded bump on the skin.

Xanthophore A cell containing yellow, orange, or red pigments.

Yolk A large sac containing stored nutrients; found in the embryos of fish, amphibians, reptiles, and birds.

INDEX

FURTHER READING

Behler, J. L., and King, F. W. 1979.
    *The Audubon Society Field Guide to North
    American Reptiles and Amphibians.*
    New York: Alfred A. Knopf.

Cogger, H. G., and Zweifel, R. G., eds. 1998.
    Encyclopedia of Reptiles and Amphibians, 2nd ed.
    San Diego, CA: Academic Press.

Conant, R., and Collins, J. T. 1998.
    *A Field Guide to Reptiles and Amphibians of
    Eastern and Central North America,* 3rd ed.
    expanded. Boston: Houghton Mifflin.

Duellman, W. E., and Trueb, L. 1994.
    Biology of Amphibians. New York: McGraw-Hill.

Halliday, T., and Adler, K. 2002.
    Firefly Encyclopedia of Reptiles and Amphibians.
    Buffalo, NY: Firefly Books.

Hofrichter, R., ed. 2000.
    *Amphibians: The World of Frogs, Toads,
    Salamanders, and Newts.* Buffalo,
    NY: Firefly Books.

O'Shea, M., and Halliday, T. 2002. *Reptiles and
    Amphibians.* New York: Dorling Kindersley.

Semlitsch, R. D., ed. 2003. *Amphibian Conservation.*
    Washington, DC: Smithsonian Institution Press.

Stebbins, R. C. 1985. *A Field Guide to
    Western Reptiles and Amphibians,* 2nd ed.
    Boston: Houghton Mifflin.

___, and Cohen, N. W. 1995.
    A Natural History of Amphibians.
    Princeton, NJ: Princeton University Press.

PHOTOGRAPHY

Cox, J. 2003. *Digital Nature Photography.*
    New York: Watson Guptill/Amphoto.

McDonald, J. 1998. *The New Complete
    Guide to Wildlife Photography: How to
    get close and capture animals on film.*
    New York: Watson Guptill/Amphoto.

Shaw, J. 2000. *John Shaw's Nature Photography Field
    Guide.* New York: Watson Guptill/Amphoto.

INTERNET

American Museum of Natural History
http://research.amnh.org/herpetology/index.html
General information on amphibians and reptiles.
Up-to-date list of all the world's amphibian species,
with details on taxonomy.

AmphibiaWeb
http://elib.es.berkeley.edu/aw/
Comprehensive information on amphibian biology
and conservation.

Animal Diversity Web
http://animaldiversity.ummz.umich.edu/site/index.html
University of Michigan online database of animal
natural history, distribution, classification, and
conservation biology.

Frogwatch USA
http://www.nwf.org/frogwatchUSA/
A long-term frog and toad monitoring program
managed by the National Wildlife Federation in
partnership with the U.S. Geological Survey to
collect information about frog and toad populations
in the U.S.

Nature Serve
http://www.natureserve.org/explorer/
Encyclopedia of plants and animals and their habitats
in North America.

Web Interactive Frog Dissection Tutorials:
Frog Net_http://curry.edschool.Virginia.EDU/go/frog/

Virtual Dissection Kit_http://froggy.lbl.gov/virtual/

http://www.froguts.com

PICTURE CREDITS

Page 1 © John Netherton; 2 top © David A. Northcott/ CORBIS; 2 bottom, 3 top © John Netherton; 3 bottom © Michael & Patricia Fogden/CORBIS; 4 © John Netherton; 6–7 © David Northcott 4390; 8 © Lynda Richardson/CORBIS; 9 © Joe McDonald/CORBIS; 10 © Michael Prince/CORBIS; 11, 12–13 © John Netherton; 14 © Joe McDonald J1AM1-00040; 15 © John Netherton; 16 © John Sibbik; 17 © Michael & Patricia Fogden/CORBIS; 18 © Lynda Richardson/CORBIS; 21 top © Daniel Heuclin/NHPA; 21 bottom left © Joe McDonald J1AM1-00637; 21 bottom right Kevin Schafer/ CORBIS; 22 top and bottom © John Netherton; 23 left © Theo Allofs/CORBIS; 23 right © Nigel J. Dennis; Gallo Images/CORBIS; 24 top left and right © John Netherton; 24 bottom left courtesy American Museum of Natural History, New York; 24 bottom right © John Netherton; 25 top © Zig Leszczynski/Animals Animals; 25 bottom © John Netherton; 26 top © Elizabeth Parer-Cook & David Parer/AUSCAPE; 26 middle courtesy American Museum of Natural History, New York; 26 bottom and top left © John Netherton; 27 bottom © Joe McDonald J1AM1-00631; 28 top © Raymond Mendez/Animals Animals; 28 bottom © Bettmann/CORBIS; 29 © John Netherton; 30 © John Tinning; Frank Lane Picture Agency/CORBIS; 31 © Michael & Patricia Fogden/CORBIS; 32 © Jay Dickman/CORBIS; 33 top left © Roger Wilmshurst; Frank Lane Picture Agency/CORBIS; 33 top right © Joe McDonald/CORBIS; 33 middle © John Netherton; 33 bottom © Kevin Schafer/CORBIS; 34 © Michael & Patricia Fogden/ CORBIS; 35 © Michael & Patricia Fogden/CORBIS; 36–37 © John Netherton; 39 © Martin B. Withers; Frank Lane Picture Agency/CORBIS; 40, 41, 42 © John Netherton; 43 bottom © Gianni Dagli Orti/CORBIS; 44 top © David A. Northcott/ CORBIS; 44 bottom © B. Borrell Casals; Frank Lane Picture Agency/CORBIS; 45 © Michael & Patricia Fogden/CORBIS; 46 © David Aubrey/CORBIS; 47 © John Netherton; 48 © David A. Northcott/CORBIS; 49 © Neil Miller; Papilio/ CORBIS; 50 © Howard Friedman; 50 inset © Michael & Patricia Fogden/CORBIS; 51 © Joe McDonald J1AM1-0043; 52 © Michael & Patricia Fogden/CORBIS; 53 © Zig Leszczynski; 54 © Kevin Schafer/CORBIS; 55 top © David A. Northcott/ CORBIS; 55 bottom © William Flaxington; 56 © Buddy Mays/ CORBIS; 57 top courtesy Australian Government, Dept. of the Environment and Heritage; 57 bottom © John Netherton; 58 © D. Alamany & E. Vincens/CORBIS; 59 top © J. M. Storey, Carleton University; 59 bottom left © Tim Wright/CORBIS; 59 bottom right © Dr. Jack Layne/Slippery Rock University of Pennsylvania; 60 © W. Perry Conway/ CORBIS; 61 © E. Jonathon Blair/CORBIS; 63, 64 top © John Netherton; 64 bottom © Joe McDonald/CORBIS; 65 top © Michael & Patricia Fogden/CORBIS; 65 bottom © Joe McDonald J4AM1-00022; 66 left © John Netherton; 66 right © Thomas Villegas, www.pumilio.com; 67 top Lydia Fucsko/frogs.org.au; 67 bottom © John Netherton; 68 top Lydia Fucsko/frogs.org.au; 68 bottom © Joe McDonald J3AM1-00019; 69 top Lydia Fucsko/frogs.org.au; 69 bottom © Joe McDonald/CORBIS; 70–71 © Joe McDonald J3AM1-00070; 72 © John Netherton; 73 © Luis A. Coloma; 74 © Wildlife Heritage Trust, Sri Lanka; 75 © Howard Friedman; 76 © S. D. Bijou; 77 © Dr. B. Ackeret; 78 © David Northcott FROG-12329-13; 79 © Brad Moon; 80 © Bill Meng WCS; 81 top © Michael & Patricia Fogden/CORBIS; 81 bottom © Philip Greenspun; 82 top © Eric and David Hosking/CORBIS; 82 bottom © John Netherton; 83 top © Michael & Patricia Fogden/CORBIS; 83 bottom, 84 top and bottom right © John Netherton; 84 bottom left Dennis DeMello WCS; 85 top © Michael & Patricia Fogden/CORBIS; 85 bottom © John Netherton; 86 © Michael & Patricia Fogden/CORBIS; 87–91 © John Netherton; 92 © B. Borrell Casals; Frank Lane Picture Agency/CORBIS; 93 © Dr. Miguel Vences; 94 top © Vincent Carruthers; Gallo Images/CORBIS; 94 bottom, 95 © John Netherton; 96 left © David Northcott FROG-12085-12; 96 right, 97 top left and right © John Netherton; 97 bottom © Joe McDonald J1AM1-00186; 98, 99 © John Netherton; 100 top © David Northcott 4390; 100 bottom, 101 top © John Netherton; 101 bottom © David Northcott FROG-12173-06; 102 © David M. Green; 103 top © Phil Bishop; 103 bottom left © Ross Nolly; 103 bottom right © Phil Bishop; 104 top © David Northcott 3752; 104 bottom © David Northcott 3971; 105 top Bill Meng WCS; 105 bottom © John Netherton; 106 top © David Northcott FROG-12126-09; 106 bottom © David Northcott FROG-12062-12; 107 © John Netherton; 108 top © David Northcott FROG-12400-06; 108 bottom left © John Netherton; 108 bottom right © David Northcott 11708; 109 top © John Behler; 109 bottom left © John White; 109 bottom right © John Netherton; 110 top © David Northcott FROG-12336-19; 110 bottom © Brad Maryan; 111 top © Jeff LeClere; 111 bottom © Joe McDonald J1AM1-00249; 112 © Francesc Muntada/CORBIS; 113 top © John Netherton; 114 top © Cesar L. Barrio Amoros; 114 bottom © Axel Kwet; 115 top © John Netherton; 115 bottom © Joe McDonald J1AM1-00127; 116 top © Rod Patterson; Gallo Images/CORBIS; 116 bottom © C. Perry Conway/CORBIS; 117 top left, top right, middle, bottom left © John Netherton; 117 bottom right © Vincent Carruthers; Gallo Images/CORBIS; 118 © David Northcott FROG-12055-01; 119 top © David Northcott FROG-12417-12; 119 middle © Jeet Sukumaran; 119 bottom D. DeMello WCS; 120 bottom © Michael & Patricia Fogden/ CORBIS; 120 top © Joe McDonald J1AM1-00621; 121 © David Northcott 14992; 121 bottom courtesy www.silhouette-island.com; 122 © Raymond Gehman/CORBIS; 124 © Stephen Richards; 125, 126 © Michael & Patricia Fogden/ CORBIS; 128 © Larry Williams/CORBIS; 130 © Alison Wright/ CORBIS; 131 © Pierre Fidenci; 132 © John Netherton; 133 © Michael & Patricia Fogden/CORBIS; 136 © Joe McDonald J1AM1-00158; 148, 158 © John Netherton.

ACKNOWLEDGMENTS

The authors wish to thank the family of the late John Netherton, whose marvelous frog photographs spurred Barnes & Noble Publisher Barbara Morgan to look for someone to write a popular book on these fascinating amphibians. We would also like to express our sincere appreciation for the efforts of Barbara and designer Richard Berenson to expand the search for photos to illustrate all 30 families of frogs as well as exciting newly discovered species. No one person in their lifetime could hope to photograph representatives of all the living frogs. Additionally, we would like to thank Darrel Frost of the American Museum of Natural History's Department of Herpetology for his assistance. Dr. Frost's "Amphibian Species of the World" taxonomic database, as well as the wealth of information on amphibian biology and conservation provided by the "AmphibiaWeb" Team, directed by Dr. David Wake, University of California, provided inspiration, important direction, and greatly facilitated our mission.

METRIC EQUIVALENTS CHART

Inches to Millimeters and Centimeters

MM=Millimeters   CM=Centimeters

Inches	MM	CM	Inches	CM	Inches	CM
1/8	3	0.3	9	22.9	30	76.2
1/4	6	0.6	10	25.4	31	78.7
3/8	10	1.0	11	27.9	32	81.3
1/2	13	1.3	12	30.5	33	83.8
5/8	16	1.6	13	33.0	34	86.4
3/4	19	1.9	14	35.6	35	88.9
7/8	22	2.2	15	38.1	36	91.4
1	25	2.5	16	40.6	37	94.0
1-1/4	32	3.2	17	43.2	38	96.5
1-1/2	38	3.8	18	45.7	39	99.1
1-3/4	44	4.4	19	48.3	40	101.6
2	51	5.1	20	50.8	41	104.1
2-1/2	64	6.4	21	53.3	42	106.7
3	76	7.6	22	55.9	43	109.2
3-1/2	89	8.9	23	58.4	44	111.8
4	102	10.2	24	61.0	45	114.3
4-1/2	114	11.4	25	63.5	46	116.8
5	127	12.7	26	66.0	47	119.4
6	152	15.2	27	68.6	48	121.9